# THE KNACK

# THE **KNACK**

## THE ILLUSTRATED ENCYCLOPEDIA OF HOME IMPROVEMENTS

Volume 1

Marshall Cavendish · London & New York

## STAFF

**Editors**
Martin Preston
Richard Chapman

**Editorial Secretary**
Sue Ashby

**Art Editors**
Maggi Howells
Jonathan Alden

**Staff Photographer**
Ray Duns

**Deputy Editor**
Martin Derrick

**Projects**
Alan Cornish
Clive Padget

**Projects Editor**
Andrew Kemp

**Picture Research**
Anne Lyons

**Senior Sub Editor**
Brenda Marshall

**Production Executive**
Robert Paulley

**Sub Editors**
Barry Milton
Trevor Morris
Gregor Ferguson
Tom Hibbert
John Ward

**Production Controller**
Patrick Holloway

**Editorial Assistant**
Jill Wiley

**Designers**
Lee Thomas
Shirin Patel
Christina Fraser
Chris Legee

**Cover Design**
Jim Bamber

**Technical Consultant**
George Smith

**Production Secretary**
Linda Mifsud

**Technical Artist**
Antonio Toma

## Reference Edition published 1986

©MCMLXXX MCMLXXXI MCMLXXXII
Marshall Cavendish Limited
58 Old Compton Street
London W1V 5PA

Printed and bound in Hong Kong by Dai Nippon Printing Company

ISBN 0 85685 999 0 (Set)
ISBN 0 85685 975 3 (Vol 1)

The Knack
1. Dwellings—Remodeling—Amateurs'
manuals
I. Chapman, Richard
643'.7      TH4816

ISBN 0-85685-999-0

# Introduction

A home should be a constant source of pleasure and relaxation, but for many people, it can become a worrying liability. Pipes burst, paintwork fades, roofs leak, masonry crumbles, electrical equipment goes awry — all these jobs can cost a great deal of money when you have to call in the professionals.

**The Knack** equips you to deal with all these typical DIY tasks, as well as providing you with an endless source of inspiration for decorating and design ideas.

Using clear, step-by-step colour pictures and easy-to-follow instructions, **The Knack** teaches eight major skills courses — decorating; carpentry; plastering; plumbing; roofing; masonry; electrics; heating and ventilation. In addition, it provides three other major strands:

> *Repairs and renovations* will be a constant resource for the know-how needed to keep your home running smoothly. Also, when a crisis occurs, you'll find this a complete reference for handling emergency repairs.
>
> *The home designer* section has the latest ideas on how to make your home both beautiful and comfortable. It is good design sense that lifts your home out of the ordinary, and gives it an extra dimension, a sense of definite style.
>
> *The projects* are specially commissioned for **The Knack**, and offer a wide variety of exciting DIY projects with really ingenious ideas such as making a custom built bedhead; a smart hi-fi unit or an office under the stairs. Most can be tackled by relatively inexperienced handymen, and they certainly help to improve the home.

*\*Clear, detailed instructions for beginners* Beginners will welcome **The Knack**, because, unlike some DIY manuals, it does not assume that you have extensive prior knowledge of the subject. Instead it introduces each new fact in clear text and illustration so that you can readily grasp the principles — even if you've never held a hammer! You can read an article — on tiling a wall for example — and start to work at once. Nobody should be without this essential guide to maintaining, repairing and improving the home. Nowhere will you find such concise information and expertise in one superbly collated work.

*\*Fully planned reference* **The Knack** is one of the most complete authoritative reference works available on the subject, and is carefully planned in its arrangement to develop skills progressively — from the basics to more advanced techniques.

*\*For the more experienced* Because **The Knack** is a progressive manual, it will also appeal to the more experienced DIY enthusiast. You can utilize your experience to tackle a wide range of jobs and projects, including advanced work such as parquet flooring; hanging wall fabrics; making furniture; dry-wall plastering; pipe installation; slating and tiling roofs; installing a stone fireplace; rewiring the house and adding double glazing for insulation.

*\*Expert* The preparation of **The Knack** has enlisted the skills of a wide range of expert contributors. Decorating supply companies, tool manufacturers, hardware suppliers and technical authors have all supplied their knowledge. In addition, a reliable team of DIY enthusiasts who have learned their skills the hard way have passed on their invaluable advice and tips.

*\*Thousands of pictures for easy reference* All the expertise in the world would be useless without a good system to communicate it well. **The Knack** is specially designed for easy reference, and is lavishly illustrated with clear photographs and carefully labelled diagrams — many of them in a useful 'exploded' style for a complete overview. It is just as if you had an expert looking over your shoulder as you work!

**The Knack** will help you to improve your home dramatically, and maintain it in first class condition. You'll find it easy to carry out repairs and keep running costs down. **The Knack** is a DIY reference work of incomparable value, an indispensable home resource for years to come.

The contents list that follows will give a general idea of the enormous scope of **The Knack**. The numbers refer to the volume in which that entry can be found.

# DECORATING

Ideas for wallpaper borders    1
Decorating with tiles    1
Making the most of your
   windows    1
Wallpaper without fuss    1
Painting interior woodwork    1
Dress up your doors    1
Come alive with colour    2
Mix and match    2
Papering ceilings    2
Liven up your ceilings    2
On reflection    2
Floor finishes    2
Creative ceilings    3
Laying carpets    3
Creative carpets    3
Using plants    3
What to put up on your walls    3
How to hang curtains    3
Fitting covings    4
Halls, stairs and landings    4
Papering a stairwell    4
Preparing a floor for tiling    4
Laying floor tiles and sheet
   vinyl    4
Co-ordinate for style    4
Painting walls and ceilings    4
Achieving a style    5
Choosing wall coverings    5
Papering awkward corners    5
Choosing carpets    5
Painting exterior wood and
   metal    5
Exciting exteriors    6
Laying stair carpets    6
Decorative shutters    6
Levelling a concrete floor    6
Laying quarry tiles    7
Decorative accessories    7
Texture pointing    7
Using wood    7
Designing a spare room    7
Working with acrylic    8
Tiles with style    8
Working with glass    8
Choosing blinds    8
Hanging wall fabrics    8
Using wallpaper creatively    8
Unusual wallpapers    9
Laying wood flooring    9
Choosing curtains    9
Using fillers and primers    10

Using synthetic foam    10
Furnishing on a budget    10
Decorating with flowers    10
Making decorative mouldings    11
Choosing shelf systems    11
Polystyrene ceiling tiles    11
Painting outside walls    11
Making the most of a
   fireplace    12
Spray painting    12
Furnishing with fabrics    12
Staining and varnishing    12
Ways with windows    12
The Victorian look    13
Maintaining brushes and
   rollers    13
The modern look    14
Decorating with cork    14
Interior doors    14
Five cork projects    14
Making the most of alcoves    14
Working with glassfibre    15
Creating with glassfibre    15
The English country look    15
Wall cladding    16
Fitting a suspended ceiling    16
Mosaic tiling    16

Paint defects    1?
Room dividers    18
Interior stone cladding    18
Collections and treasures    18
Unusual wallcoverings    19
Simple wall transfers    19
Illusions of space    19
Stencils and murals    20
The oriental look    20
Putting up guests    21
Leaded lights and stained
   glass    2?
Pictures, posters and
   photos    2?
Paints and varnishes    22
Glass in the home    22
Unusual floor coverings    22
Stripping paint    22
Marbling and brush graining    22
Concealed lighting    22
Laying rubber flooring    22
Bare brick and stone
   indoors    23
Making good    2?
Disguising indoor eyesores    2?
More storage ideas    2?

# CARPENTRY

Squaring-up, sawing and
   sanding    1
Fixing wood to wood    1
Glueing and cramping    1
The art of planing    2
Using a chisel    2
All about hinges    3
Fixing to walls    3
Working with chipboard    4
Using sheet covering    4
Making halving joints    5
Saws with special uses    6
Mortise and tenon joints    6
Making mitre joints    6
Make your own mitre tools    6
A guide to door hinges    8
Designing frame furniture    8
All about wood    8
Designing box furniture    8
Working with laminates    9
Building a stud wall    9
Designing shelf systems    10
Simple ornament shelves    10
Working with cane    10
Making a cane table    10
Making dove-tail joints    11
Working with veneer    11
Erecting a close-boarded
   fence    12

Tool maintenance    12/13
Staining and varnishing    12
Bending wood    13
Home workshops    13
Build a steam box    13
Make a saw vice    13
Make a staircase    13
Fitting a wardrobe kit    16
Basic woodcarving    16
More woodcarving    17
Making window frames    17
Carving in the round    17
A carved owl    17
Boxing-in    18
Antique furniture
   restoration    19

More staircase building    20
Antique furniture
   restoration    20
Grooving and rebating    21
Demolishing timber framed
   walls    21
Interior doors    21
Making drawers    22
A small chest of drawers    22
Off the shelf windows    23
A basic DIY tool kit    23
Building a mitring jig    23
Marquetry and parquetry    23
Using a work bench    23
Tool storage unit    23

# PLUMBING

Understanding your water
   system    1
Working with copper pipe    1
Install an outside tap    2
Using a blow-lamp    2
Bending copper pipe    2
Using flexible pipe    2
When a tap leaks    3
Above-ground drainage    3
The drains underground    4
Renewing your guttering    5
Planning a shower    5
Joining copper to lead    6
Plumbing with plastics    7
Plumbing in a washing
   machine    7
Taps, valves and stopcocks    9
Types of tap    9
Laying drains    9

Dealing with damaged
   gulleys    12
Cold water systems    13
Installing a heated towel
   rail    14
Dealing with hard water    14
Repairing a WC    15
Protecting your pipework    15
Repairing an inspection
   chamber    15
Inspection chamber    16
Solving drainage problems    17
Direct water systems    18
Air locks and water hammer    19
Cesspits and septic tanks    20
Garden drainage    21
Installing a waste disposal
   unit    21
Converting water heating
   systems    23

# MASONRY

| | | | |
|---|---|---|---|
| Basic bricklaying | 1 | Removing a chimney breast | 12 |
| On a firm footing | 1 | Dry stone walling | 13 |
| An open bond wall | 2 | Shuttering concrete | 13 |
| Turning a corner | 2 | Building stepped | |
| Knocking a hole in a wall | 2 | foundations | 13 |
| Laying raft foundations | 3 | Reinforcing concrete | 14 |
| Build a garden screen wall | 4 | Removing a fireplace | 14 |
| Basic block building | 4 | Building brickwork arches | 14 |
| Which concrete? | 5 | Building a fireplace and | |
| Repointing brickwork | 6 | chimney | 15 |
| Building a house extension | 6/7 | Rendering a wall | 16 |
| Laying load-bearing | | Stone fireplace kits | 17 |
| foundations | 6 | Opening up a fireplace | 18 |
| Cavity walls to the DPC | 7 | Simple demolition | 19 |
| Lay a brick path | 7 | Air bricks | 19 |
| Damaged brickwork | 9 | Demolishing a chimney stack | 21 |
| Demolishing load-bearing | | | |
| walls | 9/10 | | |

# ELECTRICS

| | |
|---|---|
| Electricity in the home | 2 |
| Wire a plug | 2 |
| Understanding the wiring | 3 |
| An extra light in the ceiling | 3 |
| Lighting for kitchens and bathrooms | 4 |
| All about sockets | 4 |
| A spur from the ring main | 4 |
| Light up your house number | 5 |
| Light switches | 6 |
| Persistant fuse blowing | 7 |
| Lighting outdoors | 8 |
| Installing fixed appliances | 8 |
| Install a 30amp supply | 9 |
| Installing fluorescent lights | 9 |
| Concealed ceiling lighting | 9 |
| Installing a burglar alarm | 11 |
| Channelling electric cables | 13 |
| Time switches | 16 |
| Re-wiring | 17 |
| Emergency tool box | 17 |
| Outdoor electrics | 18 |
| Doorbell systems | 19 |
| Spot and track lighting | 21 |

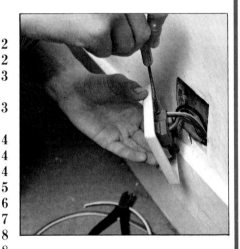

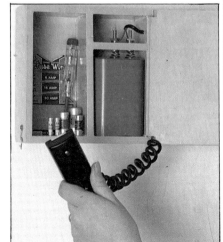

# METALWORK

| | |
|---|---|
| Hi-tech standard lamp | 11 |
| Hi-tech table lamp | 12 |
| Basic metalwork | 18 |
| Shaping metal | 19 |
| A metal clock case | 19 |
| Tubular steel frame tables | 19 |
| Simple joining techniques | 20 |
| A lightweight camera case | 20 |
| Making a terrarium | 21 |
| Soldering and brazing | 21 |
| Arc and gas welding | 22 |
| A steel framed sofa | 23 |

# ROOFING

All about roofs 4
Roof safety 5
Renewing your guttering 5
Erecting scaffolding 7
Repairing tiled roofs 8
Fascias, bargeboards and
  soffits 9
Repairs to a slate roof 11
Building a flat roof 11/12
Dealing with damaged gulleys 12
Installing a roof window 12
Repairing flashings 13
Building a lean-to pitched
  roof 13
Roofing with PVC sheet 14
Converting a flat roof 17
Installing a dormer window 20
Working with corrugated
  iron 20
Flat roof repairs 22
Building a pitched roof 24

# PLASTERING

First steps in plastering 2
Using plasterboard 10
Plastering a brick wall 10
More dry lining systems 14
Plastering an arch 15
Tanking in 21
Making good 24

# HEATING AND VENTILATION

Keeping the heat in 1
Insulate your loft 1
Ventilation in the kitchen 2
Fitting an extractor fan 2
Fitting an extractor hood 2
Maintaining central heating 3
Draught proofing 3
All about double glazing 5
Ventilation in the bathroom 7
Installing central heating 10/11
Choosing a solid fuel fire 15
Underfloor insulation 15
Air conditioning 16/17
Central heating control
  systems 18
Prefabricated chimneys 24

# EMERGENCIES

When a pipe bursts 1
Mend a fuse 2
Clearing blocked sinks and
  waste traps 3
Rodding the drains 4
Dealing with stains 5
Persistant fuse blowing 7
Protecting your pipework 15
Solving drainage problems 17
Emergency toolbox 17
Air locks and water hammer 19
Fire precautions in the
  home 23
Workshop safety 24

# POWER TOOLS

Choosing an electric drill 15
Choosing drill bits 16
Make a drill tidy 16
Successful drilling 16
Build a stool 16
Circular saws and jigsaws 17
Advanced power sawing 18
Power sanding 19
Using routers 19
A decorative book shelf 19
Planers and shapers 20
Lathes and lathework 21
Concreting tools 22
Home hiring 22
Wood turning on a lathe 23

# REPAIRS AND RENOVATIONS

Face lift for furniture                 1
Stencil magic                           1
Gutter repairs                          1
Skirting trouble                        2
Fixing floorboards                      2
When a tap leaks                        3
Maintaining central heating             3
Dealing with damp                       3
Stair problems solved                   3
Repairing fences                        4
Fitting covings                         4
Repairing carpets                       5
Dealing with dry rot                    5
Dealing with woodworm                   5
Re-pointing brickwork                   6
Replacing broken glass                  6
Repairing window frames                 7
Door repairs                            7
Persistant fuse blowing                 7
Defences against damp                   8
Repairing tiled roofs                   8
Stripping floorboards                   8
Repairs to floor joists                 8
Fascias, bargeboards and
  soffits                               9
Damaged brickwork                       9
Problems with tree roots                9
Using fillers and primers              10
Repairing window sills                 10
Repairs to a slate roof                11
More penetrating damp cures            12
Repairing stucco and render            12

Repairing flashings                    13
Using adhesives                        13
Cold water systems                     13
Repairing garage doors                 14
Injecting a damp-proof
  course                               14
More door repairs                      14
Repairing a WC                         15
Protecting your pipe work              15
More window frame repairs              15
Repairing an inspection
  chamber                              15
Repairing broken china                 16
Solving drainage problems              17
Soundproofing                          18
Stair balustrade repairs               18
Repairing gates                        18
Antique furniture
  restoration                       19/20
Air locks and water hammer             19
Lath and plaster repairs               19
Repairing with glass fibre             19
Air bricks                             19
Dealing with pests                     20
Re-turfing                             20
Recycling materials                    20
Demolishing a chimney stack            21
Tanking in                             21
Flat roof repairs                      22
Chain link fencing                     22
Stripping paint                        23
Fire precautions in the
  home                                 23
Upholstery                          23/24

# HOME IMPROVEMENTS

All about double glazing               5
Fitting double glazing                 5
Building a house extension           6/7
Build a car port                       9
Installing central
  heating                           10/1
Putting up a false ceiling            1
Installing a roof window              1
Choosing a porch                      1
Exterior door design                 1
Bearing your brickwork                1
Attics and lofts                      1
Home working areas                    1
Basements                             1
Drawing up plans                      1
Home extensions                       1
Installing a dormer window            2
Converting the roof space             2
Re-designing the kitchen           21/2
Building a greenhouse                 2
Re-designing the bathroom             2
Off the shelf windows                 2
Re-designing the bathroom             2
A timber framed extension             2
Building a swimming pool           23/24
Building a garden shed                24

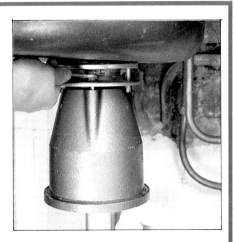

# KITCHEN PROJECTS

Stylish tiled worktop 1
Plan your kitchen 1
Flap down breakfast table 1
Fitting an extractor hood 2
Build a serving hatch 2
Modernise your kitchen 4
Streamline the sink unit 4
Dress up your doors 4
Automatic cupboard lights 4
Pine kitchen table 6
Plumbing in a washing machine 7
Pull-out storage rack 7
Build a fold away table 7
Tile top table 13
Kitchen accessories 14/15
Build a butcher's block table 19
A brick/timber kitchen system 20
Kitchen dining 21
Installing a waste disposal unit 21

# BATHROOM PROJECTS

Fitting mixer taps 1
Bathroom problems solved 1
Space-saving storage 1
Boxing in a sink 3
Planning a shower 5
Install an electric shower 5
A new look for the WC 7
Make a linen box 7
Pine bathroom accessories 12/13
Installing a heated towel rail 14
Bathrooms as living areas 23

# BEDROOM PROJECTS

Custom-built bedhead 1
Glamorous make-up unit 1
Better bedrooms 3
Make a matching bedspread 3
Build a four-poster bed 4
Elegant built-in wardrobe 5
Modern-look oak chest 5
Space-saving bed 6
Make a studio bed 7
Renovating a chest of drawers 12
A bedside cabinet 14
Build a pine bed 16
Choosing bed linen 16
Make a blanket chest 16
A colourful bed head 17
A bed head and matching screens 18
A free standing wardrobe 20
Sleeping in style 20
A bed table 20
A dressing table 20

# CHILDREN'S ROOM PROJECTS

Building a bunk bed 1
How to paint a mural 4
Planning a child's bedroom 6
A rug with a difference 6
Storage trunk for toys 8
A child's rocking chair/table 10
A traditional wooden cot 11
Nurseries 19
A child's growing chart 19
A traditional doll's house 19
Nursery furniture 21

# LIVING ROOM PROJECTS

Lighting for living rooms 1
Make your own side lights 1
Shelves with a difference 1
Simple sofa 1
Versatile coffee table 2
A feature wall mirror 2
Space saving hi-fi unit 2
Illuminated display cabinet 3
Build a bookshelf 4
Fold away corner table 4
Double-glazed patio doors 5
A revolving cabinet 6
One room living 6
Build a tea trolley 8
Decorative corner shelves 8
Comfortable lounge chair 9
Practical plinths 9
Dining rooms 9
Choosing sofas and chairs 9
Making a coffee table 9
Make a foam lounger 10

Decorative hanging light 10
Make a foam armchair 10
A corner cabinet 10
Planning a living room 11
A sideboard with style 11
A comfy seat cushion 11
Shelves for a chimney breast 12
Reclining lounge chair 12
A coffee/games table 14
A round table 15
Multi-purpose desk 15
Tables 16
A bay window seat 16
Sideboards and dressers 17
A built-in Welsh dresser 17
A room divider 17
A gate leg table 18
A design for dining chairs 19
A tubular steel frame table 19
A plywood sofa 20
A needlework table 21
A tambour-topped desk 21

A nest of tables 22
A stereo/TV unit 23
Cushions and beanbags 23
A steel framed sofa 23
A reclining chair 24
A hard wood cabinet 24

# GARDEN PROJECTS

Build a barbeque 1
An attractive stepped planter 1
An open bond wall 2
Install an outside tap 2
Dig a garden pond 2
Laying crazy paving 3
A garden incinerator 3
Build a garden screen wall 4
Repairing fences 4
Make the most of rain water 5
Planning your garden 5

Make a window box 5
Make your own paving stones 5
Light up your house number 5
Repairing paths 6
Patios 6
A rustic climbing frame 6
Lay a brick path 7
A sand pit in your garden 7
Lay a brick path 7
Front garden face lift 8
Lighting outdoors 8
Inexpensive awning 8
Plants as window decoration 9
Build a car port 9
A children's climbing frame 9
Making the most of small gardens 10
Greenhouses and conservatories 10
Decorative paving 11
Erecting a close boarded fence 12
A dustbin screen 12
A brick terraced planter 12
Dry stone walling 13
Build a dry stone planter 13
Water gardens 13

A concrete planter 14
Awnings and sun shades 15
Designing rock gardens 15
Constructing a rock garden 15
Fences and gates 15
Build a bird table 15
Walls and hedges 16
Make a sun lounger 17
Outdoor electrics 18
Garden furniture 18
Deckchair covers 18
Outdoor play areas 18
Make a wigwam 18
Returfing 20
Roof gardens 20
Chimney pot planters 21
Disguising unsightly walls 21
A garden pergola 21
Chain link fencing 22
Garden storage 22
A vegetable rack 22
Herb gardens 22
Chain link fencing 22
Rustic garden furniture 23
Sloping gardens 23
A garden swing 24
Swimming pools 24

# ADVANCED PROJECTS

Indoor/outdoor suite 1
An office under the stairs 3
Elegant divider screen 3
A telephone table/seat unit 4
A staircase storage system 5
Build your own aquarium 5
Split level floor 5
Multi-purpose storage chest 6
Build a picture window 6
Make a cane table 10
Making louvre panels 10
Storing wine 11
Putting up a false ceiling 11
Studio window conversion 11
An airing cupboard 12
Step ladder, hop-up and trestle 13
Making a staircase 14
Shelving systems 16
Fitting a suspended ceiling 16
Making window frames 17
A flap-down work table 18
More staircase building 20
An oriental style table 20
A small chest of drawers 22
A plywood dinghy 22
Make a chessboard 23

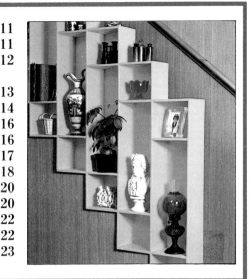

# SIMPLE PROJECTS

A simple Roman blind 1
Making a picture frame 1
Simple security 2
Build a toy truck 2
Storage ideas 2
Flexible cube storage 2
Simple stained trinket box 2
Make a rag rug 2
Make a corner planter 3
Tongue and groove panelling 3
A simple slot-in pelmet 3
Build your own work bench 3
Make a mobile 3
A tiled step feature 4
Front door peep-hole 4
A child's safety gate 4
Edging with laminates 4
Making a memo-board 5
Wall clocks from plates 5

Fit a window lock 5
Make your own mitre tools 6
Decorative shelves 6
Heat resistant teapot stand 6
Make a bread board 7
Ideas for saving space 7
Three simple lamps 7
A simple peg board 7
Make a roller blind 8
A vase 8
An odds-and-ends rack 8
A solitaire board 8
An egg rack 8
A personal writing box 8
Make a paper lampshade 8
Window display shelves 9
Versatile storage trunk 9
Make a lazy Susan 9
Simple ornament shelves 10
A frame for dried flowers 10
A hanging rack for pot plants 10

Making a collector's box 11
A new look for an old table 11
Co-ordinated table dressings 12
Making an oil-stone box 12
Free standing lamps 12
A Victorian-style picture frame 13
Cube storage system 13
Five cork projects 14
Tool box and tool carriers 14
Make a drill tidy 16
Fitting a wardrobe kit 16
Tidy up your milk bottles 16
Make a heatproof stand 16
Build a stool 16
A decorative bread board 16
Practical and pretty rugs 17
Padded picture frame 17
A handy work box 17
A carved owl 17
A tool belt and apron 17
Plant holders 17
Making a trellis divider 18
A household file 18
An unusual display shelf 18
A decorative book shelf 19
A stylish picture frame 21
Build a hall stand 21
A supportless shelf system 22
A marbled column 23
A fishing seat 23
Cushions and beanbags 23
A sledge and a cart 23
A hanging kitchen rack 24

# Metric Conversion Chart

**Length**

| | | | | | |
|---|---|---|---|---|---|
| Centimetre (cm.) | = | 0.3937 in. | Inch | = | 2.5400 cm. |
| Metre (m.) | = | 3.2808 ft. | Foot | = | 0.3048 m. |
| Metre | = | 1.0936 yd. | Yard | = | 0.9144 m. |
| Kilometre (km.) | = | 0.6214 mile | Mile | = | 1.6093 km. |

**Area**

| | | | | | |
|---|---|---|---|---|---|
| Sq. cm. | = | 0.1550 sq. in. | Sq. in. | = | 6.4516 sq. cm. |
| Sq. m. | = | 10.7639 sq. ft. | Sq. ft. | = | 0.0929 sq. m. |
| Sq. m. | = | 1.1960 sq. yd. | Sq. yd. | = | 0.8361 sq. m. |
| Hectare | = | 2.4710 acres | Acre | = | 0.4047 hectare |
| Sq. km. | = | 0.3861 sq. mile | Sq. mile | = | 2.5900 sq. km. |

**Volume**

| | | | | | |
|---|---|---|---|---|---|
| Cub. cm. | = | 0.0610 cub. in. | Cub. in. | = | 16.3872 cub. cm. |
| Cub. m. | = | 35.3145 cub. ft. | Cub. ft. | = | 0.0283 cub. m. |
| Cub. m. | = | 1.3079 cub. yd. | Cub. yd. | = | 0.7646 cub. m. |

**Capacity**

| | | | | | |
|---|---|---|---|---|---|
| Litre | = | 61.0250 cub. in. | Cub. in. | = | 0.0164 litre |
| Litre | = | 0.0353 cub. ft. | Cub. ft. | = | 28.3162 litres |
| Litre | = | 0.2199 gallon | Gallon | = | 4.5459 litres |

**Weight**

| | | | | | |
|---|---|---|---|---|---|
| Gramme (Gm.) | = | 15.4324 grains | Grain | = | 0.0648 gm. |
| Gramme | = | 0.0353 oz. | Ounce (Oz.) | = | 28.3495 gm. |
| Kilogram (Kg.) | = | 2.2046 lb. | Pound (Lb.) | = | 0.4636 kg. |
| Kg. | = | 0.00098 ton | Ton | = | 1016.04 kg. |
| Tonne | = | 0.98 ton | Ton | = | 1.01604 tonnes |

# Contents

HOME DESIGNER
**Lighting for living rooms** 4
You can completely change the character of a
room without spending a fortune
Project: Making side lamps

**Making the most of your
windows** 37
All you need to know about curtains, blinds,
sheers and pelmets
Project: A simple roman blind

**Bathroom problems solved** 65
Give the dingy areas of your bathroom a
facelift without spending a fortune
Project: Space-saving storage

**Plan your kitchen** 93
What you need to know if you are planning
your kitchen from scratch
Project: Flap-down breakfast table

PROJECT
**Build a bedhead** 10
A flexible design for an original bedhead to
liven up your bedroom
Plus: Alternative designs

**Shelves with a difference** 56
Just the thing to brighten up a dark alcove and
provide extra storage space

**Simple sofa** 78
A practical but eye-catching piece of furniture
for the living room

**Glamorous make-up unit** 106
A really substantial dressing table project for
the bedroom

REPAIRS AND RENOVATIONS
**Facelift for furniture** 16
That old chest of drawers can be given a new
lease of life by stripping off the paint and
waxing the wood
Project: Stencil ideas

**Gutter repairs** 60
How to make sure your rainwater system
keeps on protecting your home

MASONRY COURSE
**Basic bricklaying** 20
Bricklaying is not as difficult as is often
thought. Follow the step-by-step guides
Project: Build a barbecue

**On a firm footing** 88
All about building strip foundations for garden
masonry projects
Project: An attractive stepped planter

PLUMBING COURSE
**Understanding your water
system** 26
The first part of the plumbing course unravels
the mysteries of domestic plumbing systems

**Working with copper pipe** 50
All about the plumber's basic raw material,
including how to cut and join it
Project: Fitting a mixer tap shower

DECORATING COURSE
**Decorating with tiles** 30
Tiles are cheap, simple to lay and stunning in
their effect
Project: Tile topped work surface

**Wallpaper without fuss** 82
How to hang wallpaper the way the
professionals do it
Project: Ideas for wallpaper borders

**Painting interior woodwork** 111
Preparing and brush-painting your woodwork
the easy way
Project: Dress up your doors

CARPENTRY COURSE
**Squaring up, sawing and
sanding** 44
We take you step by step through these
important carpentry skills
Project: An indoor/outdoor suite

**Fixing wood to wood** 72
All about nails and screws—how to use them
and which to use where
Project: Build a bunk bed

**Gluing and cramping** 100
How to buy and handle woodworking adhesives
Project: Making a picture frame

HEATING AND VENTILATION COURSE
**Keeping the heat in** 116
A comprehensive guide to roof insulation and
cutting fuel costs
Project: Insulate your loft

# Lighting for living rooms

**Using light to create atmosphere and set the mood is one of the cheapest and most effective ways to transform a well-decorated, but otherwise lifeless room. The trick is not to go for the most obvious lighting positions**

Most of a family's life is spent in the living room—often with several people wanting to do different things at the same time. To cope with a variety of activities, the lighting system in a living room needs to be as flexible as possible.

## Making the most of ceiling lights

Usually, living rooms are equipped with a central lighting point in the ceiling. Using a traditional half-shade in this position creates a harsh, monotonous light that does nothing to show off the good points of your room, nor to disguise any less attractive features.

There are a number of ways to avoid this problem without spending a great deal of money. For instance, try extending the central flex and looping it through a ceiling hook—this gives you the scope to hang a pendant light wherever you choose, perhaps over a dining table or in a corner near a sofa.

Downlighters are another good solution for a central lighting point. Basically a downlighter is a fixed, downward-pointing spot, available in either a cylinder-shaped holder or as a special fitting designed to be recessed into the ceiling.

A central group of these recessed downlighters will provide excellent, even floor illumination, although it does mean cutting holes into the ceiling—or having a false ceiling installed —to fit them. Up to four may be wired from the same central ceiling point. They are available with varying beam widths and the wider the beam, the more light is spread over the floor area underneath.

Downlighters are especially useful for visually lowering a high ceiling and, if you can position them more freely, for highlighting coffee tables, plants and ornaments.

Any potential accident spot, such as a step-down between an open-plan lounge and dining area, will need to be constantly lit—a downlighter or spotlight is ideal for this purpose.

Spotlights provide a versatile solution to most lighting problems and if you fit a cluster of them in place of the central light, you can direct the light around the room to where it is most needed.

Spots can be aimed directly at an object for a dramatic effect—and still give an adequate general light over the rest of the room. They can be angled at walls, ceilings or mirrors to make a small room seem larger or a dark room seem brighter. You can direct light over a chair, a table or a section of the floor area where a member of the family normally reads, plays, or sits.

Where extra lighting is needed, spot lights on a ceiling-mounted track give you plenty of flexibility. The aluminium tracks come complete with ceiling mounts and all the electrical conductors are safely concealed inside. You can fit up to four spotlights to a track, providing their combined wattage does not exceed that of the power point.

Probably the cheapest way to soften the effect of a single central light is to use one of the many shapes of large, paper lamp-shades. These create a virtually glare-free, two-dimensional light. Light shining from the hole at the top of the shade bounces off the ceiling, forming a pool of brightness, while light through the shade diffuses gently over the room. However, if the effect is to be maintained the shade will need regular dusting.

Ceiling light systems can be made even more flexible by installing a dimmer switch at the main control. These are easy to fit and are wired in exactly the same way as the switch being replaced. They allow the light to be adjusted from full strength to a cosy glow with many subtle moods in between.

Before installing a dimmer switch to control several lights, check that it has the correct wattage rating. A standard dimmer will usually control up to four 60 watt or two 100 watt bulbs. Fluorescent lights need a special kind of dimmer switch, ideally installed by a qualified electrician. Plug-in dimmers are also available if y prefer a less permanent fixture.

## Wall lights and side lights
More flexible than ceiling lights combination of wall and portable lig can be tailored to suit all the fami needs.

Wall lamps provide good ba ground light but are best insta when you redecorate, as the sup wire must be chased into the wall hind the plaster. Making a feature the supply wires—with coloured sp flexing—is an alternative, decorat way of overcoming any re-wir problems.

There is an enormous range attractive wall lights to choose fro to complement all kinds of decor. alternative, however, is to make of wall mounted lights which conc the actual fittings.

Concealed strip lights—in v units, above and below book shelv under pelmets or in alcoves—are subtle source of background light and provide an attractive carpet light down the wall. Book shelves be illuminated by strip lighting fi to a batten. If necessary, you can h the batten by painting or paperin to match the wall.

Mounted strip lights can also

National Magazine Company

**Above and left:** *By simply rethinking lighting arrangements, the drab and harsh atmosphere of this open-plan living room has been transformed. Free-standing lamps and a pendent light above the table create soft pools of light, while strip lights concealed in the shelving draw attention to the ornaments*

used to highlight pictures or wall ornaments. Special fittings, which shine light against the wall but shade the direct light from the room, are ideal for this and are available from most lighting shops.

Free-standing table or shelf lamps near the wall have the same effect and, combined with standard lamps, they create a very flexible lighting system. If you want to avoid highlighting the wall, choose one of the low-level lamps with a translucent 'mushroom' shade—these cast pools of warm, subdued light down on to the table for alternating the mood of a room and are perfect for parties. Some of the larger coloured bulbs are decorative enough without a shade.

### Portable lights

There is no need to lose the subtle effect of your non-central lighting

# Home designer

Bernard Fallon

**Above**: *A portable standard lamp with adjustable spotlights, a hooded picture light and a looped pendent give this room a versatile lighting system.*

scheme when one of the family wants to read, sew, or do anything which requires a more direct light source. Portable table or standard lamps can give you a good directional light wherever it is needed but must be positioned carefully to be effective.

A desk lamp needs to shine down on to the work and not upwards into the eyes. The clamp-on type of shaded spotlight is ideal, and has the added advantage that you can move it around the room and clamp it on to any suitable edge or shelf.

Standard lamps can also be moved around easily. The kind with several adjustable spotlights on an upright base are the most versatile. Most are also adjustable for height.

**Below**: *A track carrying spotlights used to good effect to light a fairly large room. The light behind the sofa adds a dramatic flare and breaks up the linear pattern of the wallpaper*

Remember that trailing flexes can hazardous, so standards must be si as near to a plug socket as possib Child-proof sockets and safety pl are sensible deterrents to child poking objects into sockets.

## Lighting for dining

If you have open plan living a dining areas, it is often desirable 'lose' one area of the room wh using the other. Separate light systems for the living and dining si of the room are the simplest soluti and a rise-and-fall pendent light si directly over the dining table is ideal.

This creates a relaxed atmosph and concentrates light on the ta setting and the food itself. During day, the rise-and-fall pendent can raised to the ceiling to put it out o child's reach.

The regular handling of pend

*Elizabeth Whiting*

**Above:** *A couple of side lights and two ceiling spots provide all the light needed for informal entertaining in this room*

*ove: Highlighting a major feature the room such as a plant or picture s a stunning effect. In this case a ght spot has been set below a se of dried grasses*

ht shades means that they are likely get dirtier than most. Acrylic ades should be washed in warm apy water and sprayed with an anti- tic to prevent dust settling too ickly. Fabric shades need only be htly brushed to remove dust. Dirty arks on cotton shades can be re- oved by rubbing with dry bread.

Candles are the simplest and one of e most attractive ways of illumin- ng a dining table—their warm and ft light creates a romantic, friendly eling. A wide variety of shapes and es is available and you can always ake your own. All kinds of unusual lders are possible: earthenware bowls, brandy goblets, egg cups—in fact anything you like.

Candle-making kits come complete with instructions and many colours of wax, some of which are even delicately perfumed.

## Unusual lighting

There are some most unusual orna- mental lights readily available, such as the luminous, oil-in-water towers. Like a kaleidoscope, these constantly change shape within their container and at the same time illuminate a corner of the room. Obviously, these will not blend in with every living room and are not to everyone's taste, but they are a good example of the exotic dimensions lighting in a living room can take.

For a completely different effect, you could choose an antique lamp, powered either by oil or electricity. Original antique lamps will be expen- sive but there are many attractive reproductions available. Even the ordinary, camping paraffin lamps can be brightly painted to blend in with the colours of a living room. They are cheap to run and provide a gentle light which is adequate for reading by if the lamp is properly positioned.

Oil and paraffin wall lights are also widely available. Although there is usually some smell when the lamps are burning, they involve none of the fuss of rewiring and consequent redecor- ating—they need only be screwed onto the wall. And, of course, they add an attractive, old-fashioned feature to the appearance of the room.

## Choosing bulbs and shades

The right bulb or shade makes all the difference to your lighting: choosing different bulbs or a smart new shade is an inexpensive way to brighten up an existing scheme.

Shades need some careful thought before you buy—it is important to try and see a shade in the shop actually in use over a lighted bulb. This is the only sure way to see what kind of light the colour and texture of the shade is going to create. The depth of colour can be very deceptive and you may find, for example, that an open- weave basket shade creates a strong pattern on the wall, or that a heavily patterned fabric is concealing too much light for your needs.

There are some commonsense points to bear in mind when buying bulbs— the basic one is to make sure that the wattage is not too high for the shade, to avoid overheating. Besides the usual household filament bulb, there are now many different types and shapes designed for special fittings, so you may need to check with the shop that you are buying the right one. There are mushroom shapes for use with shallow fittings, a large range of reflector lamps for spots and down- lighters and all kinds of interesting ornamental bulbs for wall bracket lights.

Coloured lightbulbs can be useful too, in the standard shades of blue, red, yellow, green and pink. A simple way dramatically to change the mood in the living room, they are especially good for party lighting.

Coloured light bulbs look best when they are not used as a main light source. And it is generally true that green is relaxing, that red acts as a stimulant and that blue is a rather clinical colour.

# Make your own side lamps

Gavin Cochrane

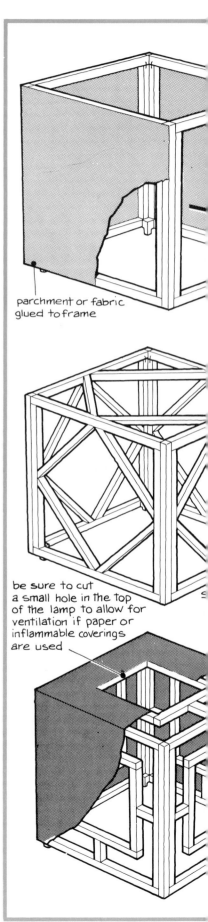

parchment or fabric glued to frame

be sure to cut a small hole in the top of the lamp to allow for ventilation if paper or inflammable coverings are used

Decorative lamps add interest to any room but can be expensive if you buy the mass-produced variety. Their purpose is to add atmosphere and a pleasing light to the room—but not necessarily to provide a strong illumination.

The designs for the cube lamps opposite and the simple bottle lamp can be put together easily and cheaply —you can modify the exact design to suit your own decor.

The cube lamps are built from inexpensive balsa wood frames with a base made from a short length of hard wood which can be varnished or painted. The covering for the frame can be any material, such as parchment, above, (available from some stationers) or fabric, right. Take care not to make the cubes too small and use a low wattage bulb (not more than 60W) or there could be a risk that the covering will scorch or even burn.

If you use very thin tissue paper, cut a hole in the top surface of the cube so that heat from the bulb can escape without scorching.

...lue and staple the balsa
...ood frames together
...nd form the basic cube
...s shown

...ts

# Lamps from storage jars

To make the bottle lamp in the picture you need a brown glass storage jar (obtainable from most hardware shops) and a small glass sphere (obtainable from florist shops for covering small plants).

Drill a hole in the side of the glass jar for the flex and fix a large bulb socket in the base with a generous daub of plasticine. Insert an upward-pointing spotlight then fit the glass sphere as shown.

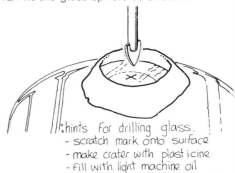

hints for drilling glass.
- scratch mark onto surface
- make crater with plasticine
- fill with light machine oil
- use hand drill and sharp bit

drill large holes allowing air to circulate

use balsa wood to build the frames to suit your own dimensions and the wattage of the bulb used.
as a guide a 60 watt bulb must have at least a 200mm sided cube around it

hardboad base to hold lampholder

make balsa wood pegs to hold frame and cube together from offcuts of side battens

hardwood frame to suit dimensions of cube

Advertising Arts

# Custom-built bedhead

Jerry Tubby

**You can build this stylish bedhead in less than a weekend for far less than the cost of the mass produced variety. The design is highly flexible so you can adapt it to fit any size of bed—or any style of bedroom**

This fitted bedhead is an attractive, easy-to-build, piece of bedroom furniture. The hinged side units are designed to hold an alarm clock, books or tissues and to incorporate lights and stereo speakers—exactly where you want them. By day, the units fold back against the wall, space saving and unobtrusive. By night, they swing round to place everything within easy reach.

The foam-padded centre section can be fitted to most beds, double or single —simply alter the stated dimensions to suit your own needs. Once in place, it forms a comfortable, colourful headrest.

Simplicity is the key to the design. The whole unit is made of laminated chipboard, one of the cheapest materials available. Once cut, each piece screws and glues together without any need for complicated woodworking joints. And the smooth finish of the plastic laminate means there is no need to prime it before painting.

The bedhead is held to the wall by screws and wall-plugs. Providing your bedroom wall is strong enough to take these types of fixing, you should have little trouble fitting the unit. And, because only the centre section is fixed, permanent marking of the wall is kept to a minimum.

All the instructions for building t bedhead are given in the accompaning diagrams. The dimensions sho in the diagrams will build the u shown in the picture above, but y can vary them to suit your ov requirements.

## Materials

For an average double bed you w need at least 1.6m² of 16-20mm ch board. However, you may have buy more if you modify the design any way or if you have a wide bed.

The centre section, which holds t foam head block is backed with 7n plywood. Match up the dimensions this section to the width of your b to work out how much plywood buy. The same goes for the foa padding—this time adding 6mm round to the basic dimensions. cutting the foam block slightly bigg than the retaining frame, it is co pressed and held firm without glu is makes it easy to remove for aning.

On the side sections the backing eaker panels are made from 3mm rdboard (buy at least 0.5m²).

The light panels are made from eet perspex, 279mm x 203mm x 3mm, d in place with magnetic catches (2 · panel). Your local stockist should able to cut these to size. You need out 4m of 12mm battening to line

the frames and hold the speaker and light panels.

You need steel chipboard screws: sixty 40mm x No 8, thirty 25mm x No 6 and a dozen 60mm x No 12. Buy plenty of 19mm panel pins and four 50mm brass hinges.

It is a good idea to match the covering material of the headrest to the bed cover. There is no need to make a fitted cover for the foam block, simply

stretch the material taut and pin and sew it firmly to the back.

You should be able to complete the construction work in a weekend, and get the first coat of paint on. Be sure to roughen up the surface of the coated chip board with glasspaper to provide a good base for the paint to key on to. Use at least three coats of paint to get a tough, hardwearing finish, sanding down lightly in between each coat.

# Suit yourself – alternative designs

The basic design of the bedhead is extremely versatile and can be adapted to suit any kind of bedroom. The swinging side units can be made in any shape you care to think of—and the cupboards and shelves within them can be arranged in almost any fashion—the units need not even be symmetrical. It all depends who sleeps on which

side of the bed and how much storage space is required.

Remember though, that the longer and wider you make the side units the greater the strain imposed on the supports and hinges—especially if you plan to use the shelves for heavy items such as books. To strengthen the overall design use extra hinges and heavy duty wall

plugs to secure the assembly to the wall. Alternatively extend the side units to the floor and mount them on castors, which will then take most of the weight. The three suggestions below show just a few of the many variations on the basic theme and by choosing natural wood rather than coated chipboard you can achieve almost any finish.

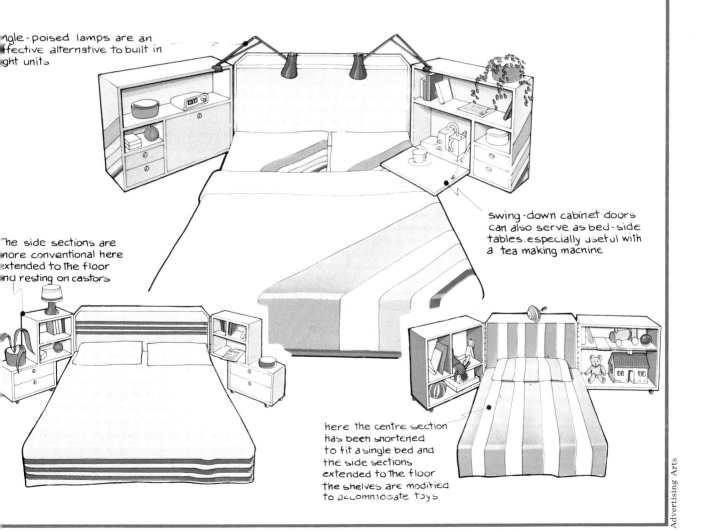

ngle-poised lamps are an ffective alternative to built in ght units

The side sections are more conventional here extended to the floor nd resting on castors

swing-down cabinet doors can also serve as bed-side tables, especially useful with a tea making machine

here the centre section has been shortened to fit a single bed and the side sections extended to the floor the shelves are modified to accommodate toys

# Workplan

The bedhead is built using a simple box frame construction without the need for complicated joints involving intricate saw cuts. However, to avoid costly mistakes there are a few important points to remember.

It is essential to pre-drill all the screw holes in the end grains of the chipboard or there is a danger that the board may split as the screw is driven home. Use shankless screws, specially designed for chipboard.

To make the joint extra strong, use an epoxy based impact adhesive as well as the screws.

To get a really accurate square corner on the boxes, cut the chipboard a few millimetres over length for the top and bottom components and plane the overhang right down flush with the side panels.

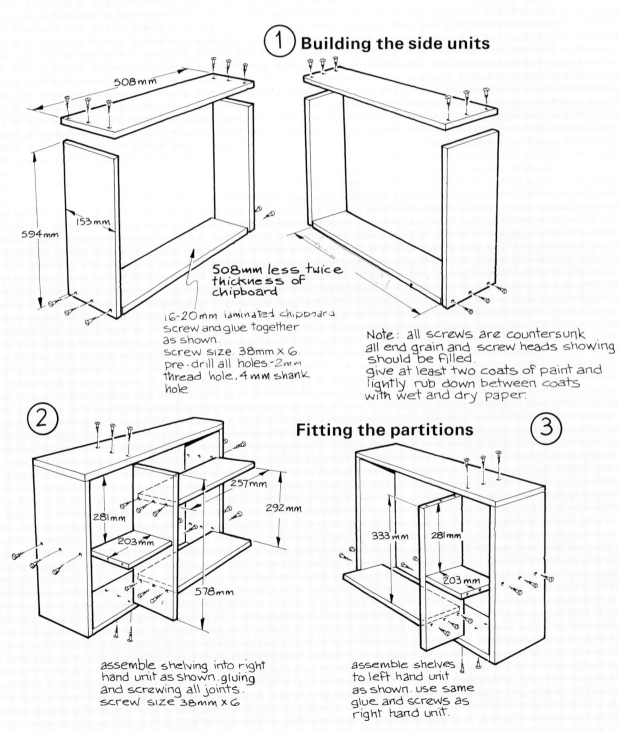

## ① Building the side units

508mm

594mm

153mm

508mm less twice thickness of chipboard

16-20mm laminated chipboard
screw and glue together
as shown.
screw size. 38mm x 6.
pre-drill all holes.-2mm
thread hole, 4mm shank
hole

Note: all screws are countersunk
all end grain and screw heads showing
should be filled.
give at least two coats of paint and
lightly rub down between coats
with wet and dry paper.

## ② 

257mm

292mm

281mm

203mm

578mm

assemble shelving into right
hand unit as shown, gluing
and screwing all joints.
screw size 38mm x 6

## Fitting the partitions ③

333mm

281mm

203mm

assemble shelves
to left hand unit
as shown. use same
glue and screws as
right hand unit.

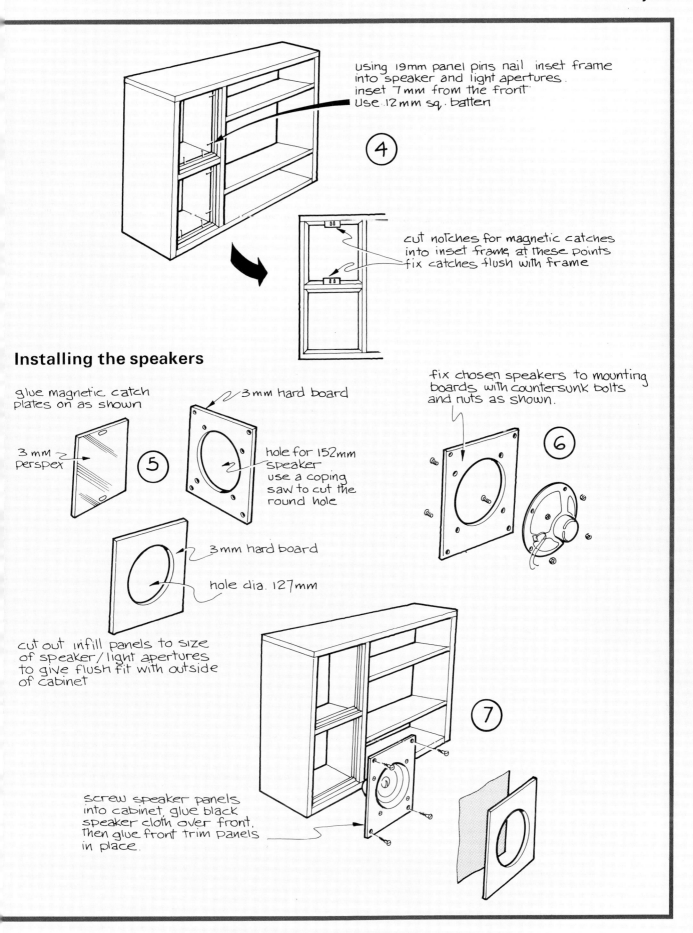

using 19mm panel pins nail inset frame into speaker and light apertures. inset 7mm from the front. Use 12mm sq. batten

④

cut notches for magnetic catches into inset frame at these points fix catches flush with frame

## Installing the speakers

glue magnetic catch plates on as shown

3mm hard board

3mm perspex

⑤

hole for 152mm speaker use a coping saw to cut the round hole

fix chosen speakers to mounting boards with countersunk bolts and nuts as shown.

⑥

3mm hard board

hole dia. 127mm

cut out infill panels to size of speaker/light apertures to give flush fit with outside of cabinet

⑦

screw speaker panels into cabinet, glue black speaker cloth over front. Then glue front trim panels in place.

# Project

## Fitting the lights

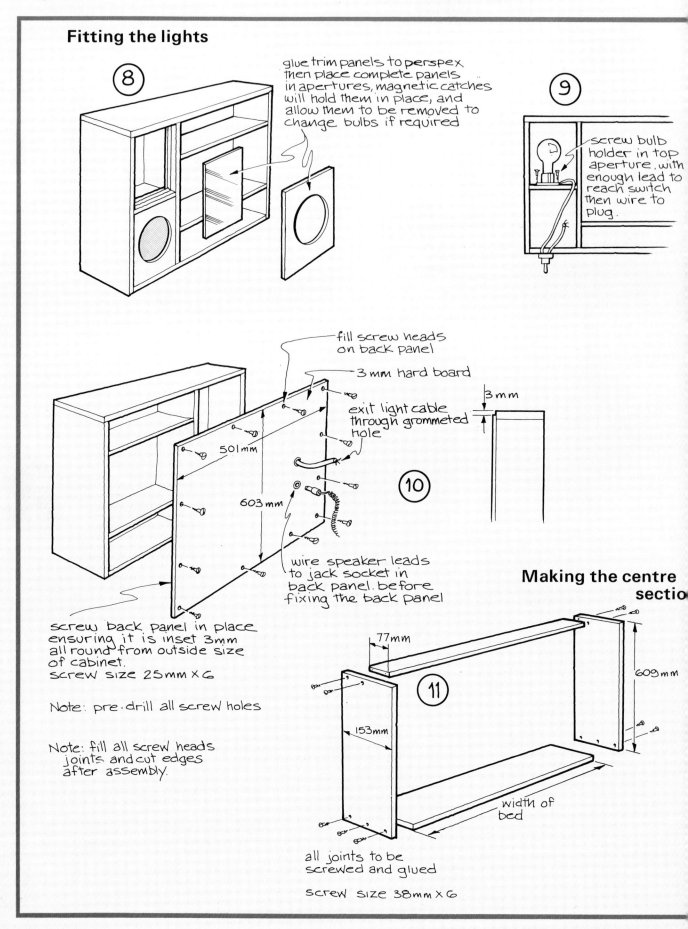

⑧ glue trim panels to perspex then place complete panels in apertures, magnetic catches will hold them in place, and allow them to be removed to change bulbs if required

⑨ screw bulb holder in top aperture, with enough lead to reach switch then wire to plug.

fill screw heads on back panel

3 mm hard board

3 mm

exit light cable through grommeted hole

501mm

603 mm

⑩

wire speaker leads to jack socket in back panel. before fixing the back panel

screw back panel in place ensuring it is inset 3mm all round from outside size of cabinet.
screw size 25mm × 6

Note: pre·drill all screw holes

Note: fill all screw heads joints and cut edges after assembly.

## Making the centre section

77mm

609 mm

⑪

153mm

width of bed

all joints to be screwed and glued

screw size 38mm × 6

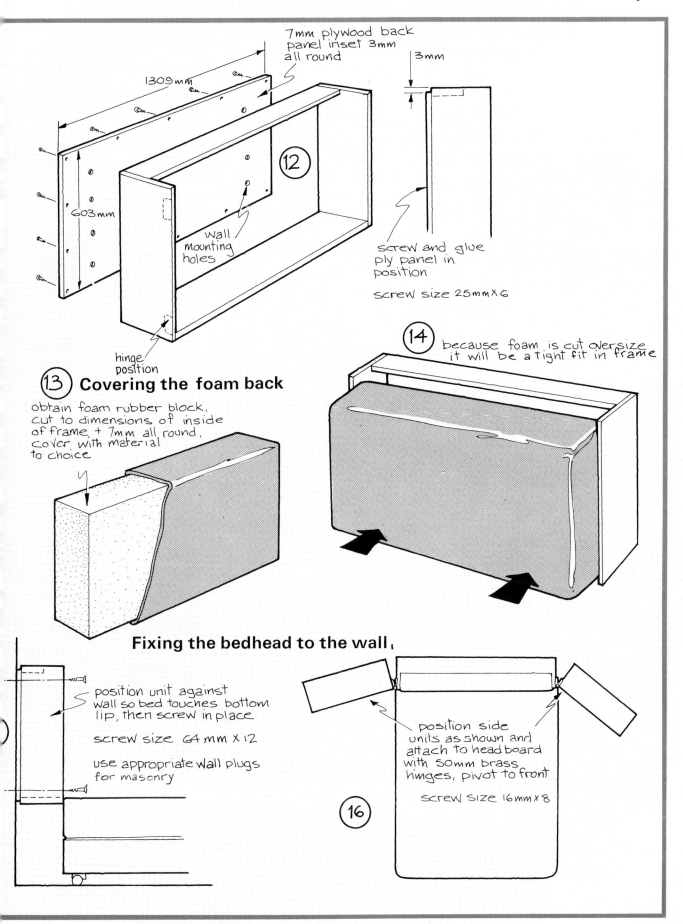

7mm plywood back panel inset 3mm all round

1309 mm

603mm

⑫

3mm

screw and glue ply panel in position

screw size 25mm × 6

Wall mounting holes

hinge position

## ⑬ Covering the foam back

obtain foam rubber block, cut to dimensions of inside of frame, + 7mm all round, cover with material to choice

⑭ because foam is cut oversize it will be a tight fit in frame

## Fixing the bedhead to the wall

position unit against wall so bed touches bottom lip, then screw in place

screw size 64 mm × 12

use appropriate wall plugs for masonry

position side units as shown and attach to head board with 50mm brass hinges, pivot to front

screw size 16mm × 8

⑯

# Facelift for furniture

## That shabby old chest of drawers can be transformed simply and cheaply by stripping off the old paint and refinishing the wood in an up-to-date, eye catching style

By stripping old furniture down to the natural wood you can ensure a smooth surface—free of bumps and blemishes—which can then be polished, varnished or even stencilled for a completely new look

Make sure, though, that you know what finish you are stripping. It could be one of several—paint, polish, lacquer or varnish—and they all need different treatments.

### Stripping paint
Paint on furniture can be removed either by immersion in a caustic bath—a job for a specialist—or by hand, using a chemical paint stripper. Hand stripping usually gives the best results, as it adds an extra lustre to the bare wood: consider the caustic bath as a last resort—only to be used if the work proves impossibly hard.

### Equipment
To strip paint by hand, you need a supply of proprietary paint stripper. Available in either jelly or liquid form, it is more economical to buy it by the gallon than to opt for one of the smaller cans. The back of the can should tell you what to wash the stripper off with once it has soaked in—either water, methylated spirits or turps substitute.

To apply the stripper, you need rubber gloves and an old 25mm or 50mm paintbrush. For peeling away the softened paint, use a stripping knife and a moulding scraper or coarse wire wool. Put the shreds—which will be caustic, and therefore dangerous—in a jam jar or an empty paint tin.

For cleaning and finishing, make sure that you have a supply of coarse wire wool and fine and medium grade glasspaper.

### Method
If you are working indoors, ensure the room is well ventilated before you start—paint stripper gives off unpleasant fumes. Put down some newspaper or an old dust sheet to protect your floor and furnishings.

On a chest of drawers start with the drawer faces themselves, removing handles and key escutcheons where possible. A dab of paint stripper, left to soak for a few minutes, will help loosen stubborn screws.

Wearing rubber gloves, pour some of the stripper into a jar and start brushing it on to the paint. Work the stripper into all the cracks and crevices with a brush making sure none of the paint is missed.

Having covered a drawer or the equivalent area, leave the stripper to act for several minutes. When the paint starts to bubble, remove the top layer with a stripping knife or a moulding scraper and scrape the shreds straight into a container.

Continue this process with each layer of paint—sometimes there are as many as five or six on an old chest of drawers—until you reach the wood. You will need several applications of stripper. If you find any corners difficult to reach with a stripping knife, use the moulding scraper instead.

When all the paint has been stripped off, the next step is to wash down the wood. This will help to remove any

**Right:** *This chest has been totally transformed into a beautiful piece of furniture, by stripping and then polishing with homemade beeswax polish*

**Above:** *A neglected, old chest covered with dirty, pitted paint can easily be stripped down to the natural wood and given a new finish*

remaining debris and also neutrali the stripper.

Follow the manufacturer's reco mendation on what neutralizer to with your particular stripper. Soal into a hand-sized wad of wire wool thoroughly rub over the stripped s faces until they are as clean as can get them.

Finally, when the wood is d

has been used before you can remove it successfully.

**French polish** gives a fine, mirror-like surface which is very delicate and easily marked by heat or liquid. The surface shine is the result of the polishing techniques rather than the ingredients of the polish.

French polish can easily be removed with methylated spirits. Wipe it on generously and then leave it for a few minutes. When the polish has softened scrape it off, first with a scraper, then with fine wire wool soaked in methylated spirits. When the wood is dry, glasspaper it down to a smooth finish.

**Wax polish and oily surfaces** can be removed by rubbing with fine steel-wool soaked turpentine or turps substitute. Dry with an absorbent rag and repeat the process until you reach bare wood.

If you are not sure what sort of polish is on your furniture, choose a small, unobtrusive part of the surface and rub real turpentine on the spot with a soft cloth. This will remove dirt and wax or oil finishes and quickly reveal bare wood. If there is polish left after applying the turpentine, rub on a little methylated spirit—if the surface has been French polished it will go soft and sticky.

**Varnished and lacquered finishes**
If your chest of drawers is more than 30 years old and is varnished, you are dealing with oil-based varnish. This is made from resins dissolved in oils and solvents and is quite different from modern cellulose and polyurethane varnishes.

The cleanest way to remove oil-based varnish is with a scraper. Tilt the scraper away from you and push it along the grain of the wood, working away from your body. Never use it across the grain.

**1** *Remove the handles from drawers if possible. Pour some stripper into a jar and apply it to the wood. Work it well into any cracks*

**2** *Leave it until the paint starts to bubble then, with a stripping knife, remove the top layer of paint. Scrape the paint shreds into a tin*

**3** *Use a moulding scraper to get the paint out of difficult corners and continue applying stripper until all paint has been removed*

**4** *Rub the bare wood with coarse wire wool dampened in turps substitute or water. When dry, rub with glasspaper to smooth it*

sspaper it down to a smooth finish. e medium grade paper to work out deeper scratches, then go over the ole surface with a fine grade. Rub the direction of the wood grain en using wire wool or glasspaper.

**ripping polish**
he chest of drawers is polished you ed to know which type of polish

# Repairs and renovations

To remove polyurethane varnishes use paint stripper. Cellulose-based varnishes can be removed with paint-stripper, acetone, cellulose thinners, ammonia, caustic soda or turpentine. You may need to test small areas first to see which works best.

### Doing repairs

Once you have stripped off all the old paint, you may find that various faults show up and that repairs are necessary before the new finish can be applied.

If the back of the chest of drawers is weak, nail some new battening on.

Any weak joints should be glued, pinned, then held in place for several hours—either with string or in a clamp. Make sure that the corners of the chest of drawers are protected from the cutting action of the string with some paper or a piece of wood.

Cracks and holes must be filled with plastic wood or a commercial non-shrinking stopper—both are available from DIY shops. You can also buy coloured fillers and stains to match the natural colour of the wood. Level filled holes with fine glasspaper. Large holes, greater than the size of a keyhole, should be plugged with a piece of similar wood cut to shape.

Make sure that the grain of the plug goes the same way as the rest of the surface, then glue it in place with a suitable adhesive.

### Finishing—with polyurethane

Polyurethane varnish gives bare wood a lustrous, hard-wearing finish which is easy to clean and maintain. As well as clear varnish, a wide variety of colours and natural wood shades are available. The clear varieties come in matt or gloss and these can be mixed.

Polyurethane can withstand heat without marking, though intense heat may eventually damage the wood underneath. It is important to l the polyurethane set: with son varieties it can take up to two wee to achieve maximum hardness.

Apply the varnish directly to t sanded wood with a paintbrush. B cause the varnish must be applied coats, it is a good idea to dilute th first with white spirit so it soaks in ar seals the wood. When the first coat dry, lightly rub it down with fine glas paper before applying the next. Subs quent coats can be diluted in the pr portion of one part white spirit three parts polyurethane to give thi ner coats which will brush on mo easily.

Before applying the coloured varie apply one coat of clear polyuretha to seal the wood or you may get patchy effect. For a matt finish, app a final coat of clear, matt polyuretha after the coloured coats.

### Finishing—with wax polish

Wax polish can either be used conjunction with polyurethane, or itself as an alternative finish. A though wax gives a warm, mellc look to the wood, it has hardly a resistance to heat and marks easily so its use should be confined to mo decorative furniture.

With polyurethane, use a proprie ary, white wax polish. After the fin coat of varnish has dried, rub over lightly with a very fine (0000) grade wire wool. Having brushed away t dust, rub in the polish with a coar rag to give an even, matt sheen.

Finally, buff up the surface with fine cloth. Successive layers of polis built up at the rate of one every tv days, will deepen and harden t finish.

For a pure wax finish, you can mal up your own beeswax polish. For th you need pure beeswax—availab from hardware shops—turps substitu and a glass jar.

Grate the beeswax with a chee grater and put it in a jam jar. Pour just enough turps to cover the wax.

Stand the jar in a pan of very h water and stir until the mixture me and forms a thick paste—on account expose the jar to a nak flame as the turps substitute is high inflammable.

Dip a clean rag in the wax and r the mixture into the clean wood su face, taking care to spread the wa evenly. Apply enough wax to soak to the grain but avoid leaving a proud of the surface.

When the wax has hardened co pletely—in about an hour—buff up t surface with a fine cloth.

**5** *Grate the beeswax, using a cheese grater, to help it melt. Then put the wax in a jam jar and add enough turpentine to cover it*

**6** *Stand the jam jar in a saucepan of very hot water and then stir the mixture until it all melts and forms a thick paste*

**7** *Put some of the beeswax polish on a rag and rub it into the surface of the wood. Finish it off with a dry, clean cloth*

**8** *If using a polyurethane finish, this can be applied directly on to the stripped wood. For the first coat, dilute the varnish with white spirit*

# Stencil magic

Bernard Fallon

**Above**: *Stencil kits, which contain sheets of designs and a sharp knife for cutting them, are available from art and craft shops or stationers. Apart from the stencil kit, you will need newspaper to protect the floor, sticky tape or drawing pins, chalk, a palette knife or blunt kitchen knife, cardboard, a stencil brush (available from art and craft shops), small cans of gloss or enamel paints and white spirit. Make sure you gather all these materials together before you start*

## How to stencil

Cut out the stencils on a flat surface such as a board, securing them with tape or drawing pins before you begin cutting out the patterns.

If you want to stencil a group of designs, arrange the stencils in patterns until you find an arrangement that you like. Lightly chalk in the pattern to get an idea of how the finished design will look.

Mix your chosen colours with a knife, using a sheet of cardboard as a palette. Fasten the stencil to the wood with clear tape, rub off the chalk and use the stencil brush to daub paint through—or if the area of the stencil is fairly large use a spray can.

With practice, you can grade colours by lightly applying a contrasting colour over the first colour at the edges of the stencil. Wait until the paint is almost dry before painting adjacent designs or you may smudge the first ones. If you make a mistake, the paint can be removed with white spirit while it is still wet.

When you have finished, clean each stencil by placing it flat on some newspaper and wiping both sides with a rag dampened in white spirit.

**Above**: *A dark background shows off brightly coloured stencils to the full*
**Below**: *More subdued designs add a touch of prettiness to this cupboard*

Ray Rathbone/Sunday Times

# Basic bricklaying

● **The basic tool kit** ● **Mixing mortar** ● **Planning a small project** ● **Cutting bricks** ● **Handling a bricklayer's trowel** ● **How to lay bricks quickly and accurately** ● **Turning corners**

Although there is no need to collect a full set of bricklayer's tools just to build a simple project, a few are essential and will stand you in good stead later on.

*Bricklaying trowel:* absolutely vital for spreading the mortar, these are available in both right- and left-handed forms.

*Spirit level:* another essential tool, make sure that you buy the 1m bricklayer's level.

*Ball of twine:* for setting out your project.

*Shovel:* for handling and mixing the mortar.

*Bucket:* for carrying materials.

*Brick hammer and bolster:* for cutting bricks.

*Measuring tape:* for checking, as the work proceeds.

## Materials

For simple projects, there is no need to go into the relative advantages and disadvantages of different types of bricks. Simply choose a brick which matches the colour and texture of your surrounding brickwork from the local builders merchant.

Always buy a few more bricks than you need: some may get damaged in transit and others are certain to be spoilt when cutting them.

As well as bricks, you need materials which go to make up mor —fine sand and cement—plus a squa of blockboard or similar material, carry the finished mix.

## Setting out

It is essential to make sure that main wall in any project runs in straight line and remains le throughout—you can do this by c structing a marker line, to indica the edge of the proposed wall. Fir tie a length of twine, at least longer than your proposed wall, round a brick. Place the brick on-s at one end of the line of the wall: two others on top to weight it, th stretch the twine out in the directi of the wall. Finally, tie the twine another brick, weight it and pull line taut. You should now have arrangement similar to that shown fig. 1. The main wall of your proj can start anywhere along it.

When you come to mark your fi course—each layer of bricks is cal

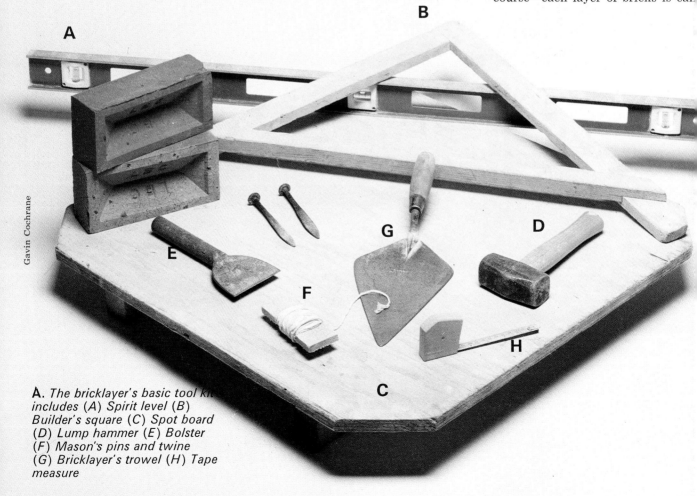

Gavin Cochrane

**A**. *The bricklayer's basic tool kit includes (A) Spirit level (B) Builder's square (C) Spot board (D) Lump hammer (E) Bolster (F) Mason's pins and twine (G) Bricklayer's trowel (H) Tape measure*

course'—your marker bricks will
aid to one side of the line, as close
it as possible without actually
hing.

n a small project, there will be no
to set out the walls which run
ight angles to the main wall: you
uld be able to judge the angles
ely enough using the spirit level as
traight edge. On larger projects,
re it is important to get corners
olutely square, more accurate tech-
es must be employed. These are
ered further on in the masonry
rse.

## king the mortar

can mix the mortar on any clean,
surface near the site. Start by
oughly mixing four shovelfuls of
with a shovelful of cement. Turn
mixture over with the shovel until
thoroughly mixed.

ext, mix up some clean, soapy
er, using washing-up liquid. The
acts as a plasticizer, binding the
tar and keeping it malleable when
come to trowel it. Form a crater
he mortar mix, then add a little of
water. Turn the mix over care-
y, adding more water as you go,
you reach a creamy consistency
et, but firm. Finally, transfer the
h mortar to your spotboard and
e it next to the baseline.

## ple bonding

order to create a rigid structure
to spread the load on any one
t, bricks are laid so that they over-
ne another or are *bonded*. The sim-
t and most common bonding style
he *half-bond* or *stretcher bond*
17). With this arrangement, the
ks in any one course overlap
se above and below by half a brick's
gth.

lways work to a pre-drawn bonding
ern: if you try to work the pattern
as you go along, you are certain to
ome confused.

## ging

successful a brick structure is
ends a great deal on the continuity
ts size or *gauge*. This not only
ies to the bricks themselves, but
to the mortar joints between them.
ideal width of a joint is 10mm. Al-
igh you may not be able to achieve
on your first course, great care
uld be taken on subsequent courses
et as close to this as possible.

n the first, bedding, course you
have to vary the thickness of the
tar slightly to take up variations
he level of your foundations.

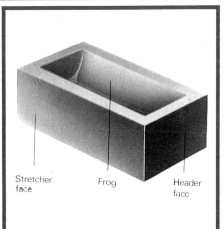

**B.** *The metric bricks now in use are made to a single, standard size*

Stretcher face · Frog · Header face

*Advertising Arts*

**1** *To set out a simple project such as our barbecue, stretch a length of twine taut between stacks of bricks and then use it as a guide line*

**2** *Before you mix any mortar, work out how many bricks need to be cut. The first step is to mark the cutting line, preferably with a gauge*

**3** *Holding the bolster exactly on the cutting line, strike it sharply to split the brick. A piece of hardboard underneath protects the patio*

## Cutting bricks

In order to achieve a proper bonding
pattern, you will inevitably be faced
with the task of cutting bricks. Start
by setting the brick on edge, on a
piece of harboard and mark a cutting
line in pencil (fig. 2). Use the edge of
the bolster to convert this into a
groove 1mm deep then position the
bolster in the groove. Finally, keeping
the bolster as near upright as possible
strike it hard with the lump hammer
(fig. 3). If the brick doesn't split at the
first attempt, do not worry—it will
eventually.

To speed up the measuring and
marking process, bricklayers use a
marking plate—three pieces of wood,
stuck together as shown in fig. 2 to
give rebates of quarter, half and
three-quarter brick sizes.

If you have a lot of bricks to cut,
it is well worth making up a plate and
cutting all the bricks before you begin
laying.

## Using the trowel

If possible, practise the knack of
handling the trowel for at least 15
minutes before you start laying any
bricks—it will save a lot of mess later
on and greatly speed up the bricklaying process.

Arrange the mortar into a neat pile
on one side of the spotboard. If you
are right-handed, the left hand edge
of your trowel as seen from above will
be a straight edge. Use this to cut a
section of mortar from the pile (fig. 4),
keeping the blade of the trowel angled
slightly towards you.

Roll the mortar down the spotboard
towards you, smoothing it to form a
sausage shape with tapering ends (fig
5). This section of mortar is known as
a *pear*. To pick it up, slide the straight
edge of the trowel under it and then
up again in a sweeping movement (fig
6). Practise doing this until you can
pick up the whole of the pear in one
sweep.

**4** To trowel a pear of mortar, start by separating a trowel-size section from the heap on the spot board. Form it roughly into shape

**5** Roll the pear down the spot board in a series of chopping movements. Practise until you can do this smoothly and quickly

**6** Pick up the rounded pear by sliding the trowel sideways— slipping it under the mortar and up again in one movement

**7** To start the first course, line up the bricks which will form the base of the main wall in a dry run. Make sure that they fit your plan

**8** Taking the brick at one end of the run as your first marker, flick a pear of mortar into the exact position you intend to lay it

**9** Before you lay the marker brick on top, flatten out the pear slightly and make a small depression so that the mortar will spread

## Marking your first course

Start by arranging the bricks which go to make up your main wall 'dry'— without mortar—along the setting-out line (fig.7). Adjust them until there is a gap of about 10mm between each one.

Take up the brick at one end and in its place, lay down a pear of mortar. Flick it off the side of the trowel to start with (fig. 8), then flatten it out to the area of a brick (fig. 9). Before you lay the brick on top, trowel a depression in the middle of the mortar to help it spread flat.

Use the spirit level to check the brick for level, making small adjustments to the brick with gentle taps of the trowel handle (fig.10). Stretch the level out along the dry run of bricks so that one end remains on the brick you have just laid. Lay the brick at the other end of the level in the same way as the first and check for level as before. Then stretch your spirit level back to the first laid brick and check to make sure that the two bricks are level with each other (fig.11).

Follow this by checking them both

**10** With the brick in place, use your spirit level to check it for true. Make small adjustments with gentle taps of the trowel handle

for line, with your level pressed against the side faces. When you are satisfied that they are in the right position, repeat the whole procedure again further on down the run, using the second, laid, brick as the level reference this time. As you stretch your spirit level down the run, make sure that the end which was on the

**11** Lay your second marker brick at the other end of the spirit level. Once it is level, match it up to the level of the first brick as sho

second brick remains there.

Continue laying marker bricks u you reach the end of the dry run. Y should end up with a series of la squared, level, marker bricks at int vals along the first course. T should be separated by a distan centre to centre, approximately eq to the length of the spirit level. O

...ll project like the one on page 24, ...will only need three marker ...cks to span the first course. Make ...nal check to ensure that they are ...level and in line with one another, ...n remove the intervening bricks.

**...ying the first course**
...rt by stretching your setting-out ...tautly along the edge of the mar... bricks (fig. 12). Use the line as a ...de for the positions of the interven... bricks. The procedure for laying ...m is as follows:
...ay down a pear of mortar
...flatten and indent it
...take up your brick, gripping it as ...wn in fig. 13
...draw off another piece of mortar, ...ut the size of a cocktail sausage
...scrape it hard against one heel edge ...he brick (fig. 13)
...do the same for the other heel edge
...lay the brick in position, against ...adjoining one
...check it with the spirit level for ...l and line
...scrape off the excess mortar and re... it to the spotboard

**...rning a corner**
...large projects, bricklayers use a ...der's square (fig. A) to help them ...ge corners correctly. For small pro... s a spirit level will suffice. Having ...your corner brick, butt the level ...against the heel of the end brick ...then tap the corner brick into line ...15).
...lternatively, you can use the ...ee-four-five' method. Measure ...r units along your main wall and ...k, then three of the same units ...g your corner brick, and mark. If ...corner is square, then the diagonal ...surement between the two marks ...t be five units.

**...ing subsequent courses**
...sequent courses of brickwork are ...in much the same way as the first. ...if you are using bricks with in... ts or frogs, allow a bit more mortar ...each pear to fill these up. As you ...down a pear, make sure you cover ...cross joint between the bricks ...w (fig 16). If a bit of mortar slips ...n, simply replace it with more.
...s you work on the second course, ...particular care to ensure that the ...ge is correct—if you lay your mor... to a depth of 12mm, this should ...en out to the required 10mm when ...ick is laid on top. Be systematic ...n your checking: as work pro... ses, you will need to check con... tly for level, line and plumb (with

**12** When you have laid all the markers, weigh down your line to touch them. Use the line to align the rest of the bricks in the wall

**13** Scrape hard as you "butter" the end of an adjoining brick— otherwise the mortar will crumble and fall off as you place the brick

**14** There is no need to check the rest of the bricks for level— just tap them into line so that they are level, but not quite touching

**15** Judge small corners such as those in our barbecue project by holding the spirit level against the end brick as a straight edge

**16** As you are laying your mortar for the second course, make sure that it completely fills in, and covers, each cross-joint on the first

**17** With a brick laid on top, the bed mortar for the second course should be about 10mm deep This shows the stretcher bond

the spirit level on end) and also that the joints are of the ideal 10mm width.

**Finishing the joints**
Finishing the joints, half an hour after they are set, will improve the overall appearance of the project and protect the mortar from erosion.

For small projects, a *round tooled*

finish is the most suitable. Bricklayers do this by scraping a special tool along the half-dry joints and then brushing away the excess mortar. But you can achieve almost as good a finish by rubbing over the joints with a piece of 12mm diameter rubber hose. Do the vertical joints first then the horizontal ones, giving priority to the latter.

# Build a barbecue

To build the barbecue you need about 300 standard size (metric) bricks, 2 bags of cement and 30kg of sand.

The seats shown are each made from 3 lengths of timber 1585mm x 75mm x 50mm, battened at either end then sanded and varnished.

A simpler alternative is to use 2 1585mm x 140mm x 50mm planks for each seat, left to rest loosely.

For the fireplate, use mild steel plate, about 450mm x 450mm x 6mm, with a piece of angle iron bolted to the front edge. Make the grille above from steel lattice of the same size. Allow a gap of 20mm all round between these and the surrounding brickwork.

Build supports into the bedding mortar to hold the plates in place. Fashion these from 25mm flat iron or 6mm mild steel dowel cut into 100mm lengths. Use 4 per plate, evenly spaced.

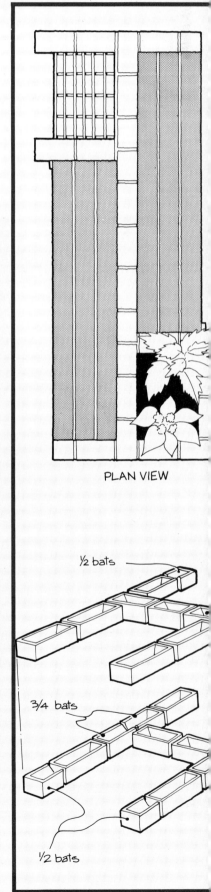

PLAN VIEW

½ bats

¾ bats

½ bats

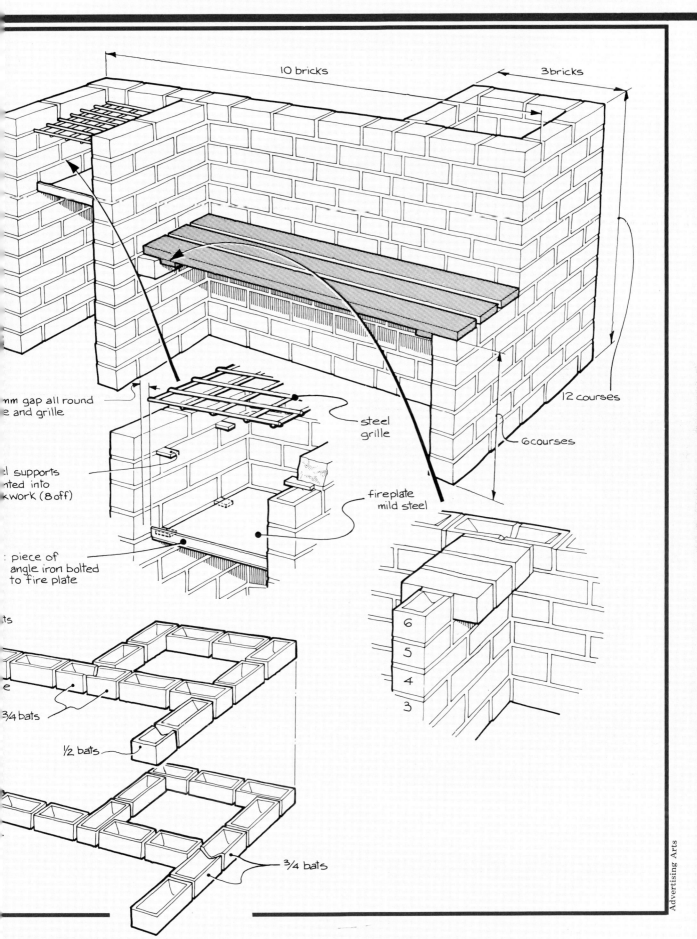

10 bricks

3 bricks

mm gap all round
e and grille

steel
grille

l supports
nted into
kwork (8 off)

fireplate
mild steel

12 courses

6 courses

piece of
angle iron bolted
to fire plate

ts

3/4 bats

1/2 bats

3/4 bats

3
4
5
6

# Understanding your water system

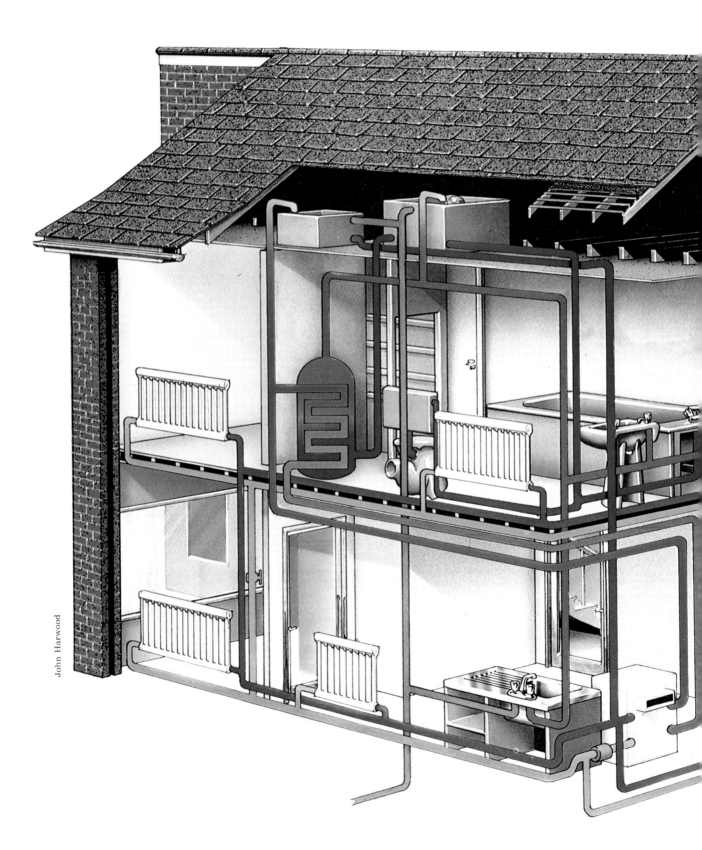

John Harwood

# The layout of most water systems is a mystery to many householders. Get to know how the plumbing system works and you will be able to save on plumbing and emergency repair bills

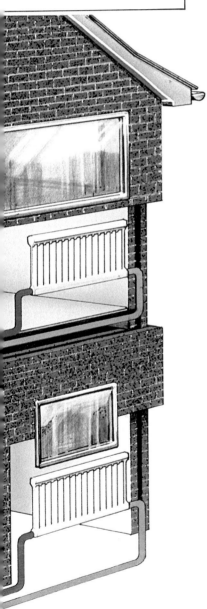

- Hot water feed to radiators
- Cooled water return from radiators
- Cooled water from heat exchanger
- Hot water feed to heat exchanger
- Rising supply main (cold)
- Cold supply from storage cistern
- Hot water supply from cylinder

**Left**: *A typical modern plumbing system incorporates two hot water loops for the hot water tank and the radiators. The water enters the house via the rising main and feeds the system from the supply tank*

Domestic plumbing systems, and the ways in which they work, often seem quite baffling. So when something goes wrong, there is always the temptation to call in a plumber, rather than venture into unknown territory.

In many cases, however, a visit from the plumber is an unnecessary expense. Although plumbing installations vary a great deal from house to house, all follow the same basic set of rules and can usually be sorted out with little difficulty.

### Where the water comes from
Cold water comes to your house from the water authority mains via a smaller, service pipe. This pipe may have been installed specifically to serve your house or you may share it with a neighbour. Either way, it will be controlled by a water authority stopcock somewhere on the edge of your, or your neighbour's property. The stopcock is sunk below ground (usually about a metre) and is encased in brickwork, concrete, or a stoneware pipe to provide access. To mark the site, a small cast-iron casing is usually fitted at ground level.

From here, the service pipe runs to your house and becomes known as the rising main. At the point where it enters, a further stopcock—known as the consumer's, or house, stopcock— is fitted. This one is your own property and, because it controls all water entering the house, it is as well to know where to find it.

The most common place is under the kitchen sink, where a branch of the rising main directly supplies the kitchen cold tap with drinking water. The other most likely locations are under the stairs, or below floorboards immediately inside the front door.

### The cold storage tank
After the branch to the kitchen cold tap, the rising main runs to a cold storage tank or cistern. The water pressure in the mains allows this to be mounted high up in the house, normally in the roof space. Older storage tanks are made of galvanized iron, which is both heavy and prone to rust. These have now been replaced by the lighter, more hygienic, plastic tanks which are maintenance-free.

The storage tank helps to iron out irregularities in the main supply and also provides an emergency reservoir if the supply is cut off.

The rising main delivers water to the top of the tank via the control of a ball-valve. At the base of the storage tank you will find the main water outlet. The stored water flows through here under the pressure of gravity and then branches off to supply the rest of your house's water requirements. These will include the lavatory, the bathroom cold taps and the hot water cylinder.

A stopcock is normally fitted somewhere near the outlet, so that you can turn off most of the water, but still leave your kitchen cold tap in operation to supply the family's needs while you are working.

### The hot water supply
In household plumbing, cold water is converted to hot either directly or indirectly. Direct heating means that the cold water comes into direct contact with a heater—normally a boiler or an electric immersion heater—then flows straight to the taps.

With indirect heating—usually combined with central heating—the water heated by the boiler is itself used to heat up fresh cold water. In this system, the two hot water circuits are separate and heat is transferred from one to the other by means of a heat exchanger.

The hot water cylinder, a copper tank heavily insulated to guard against heat loss, is common to most hot water installations.

In direct systems, it houses the electric immersion heaters—if fitted— and acts as storage tank to keep your hot water supply as constant as possible. In an indirect system, the cylinder has the additional function of housing the heat exchanger.

### The direct flow
The flow of water in both direct and indirect systems relies on the principle that hot water always rises above the cold water around it. So, in a direct system, the flow starts with cold water running to the base of the hot water cylinder.

If a boiler is fitted then the flow continues from the cylinder down to the base of the boiler. As the water is heated it rises out through the top of the boiler, up to the top (crown) of the hot water cylinder and then on to the hot taps.

If immersion heaters are fitted instead of a boiler, the flow is greatly simplified. The water runs from the storage tank to the base of the hot water cylinder and is heated: it then rises straight out of the cylinder and on to the hot taps.

The great disadvantage of direct systems is that water, when it is heated above 60°C (140°F)—or 80°C (180°F) in soft water areas—deposits scale similar to kettle fur.

The scale can block up pipework and boilers alike unless adequate precautions are taken. These include keeping the water temperature down below the 'scaling point' and using scale-inhibiting additives in your cold storage tank.

## The indirect flow
The easiest way of understanding an indirect hot water flow is to visualize two independent 'loops' of water. The first loop consists of the water used to feed the hot taps.

This flows from the cold storage tank to the base of the hot water cylinder, where it comes into thermal contact with hot water on the other loop (via the heat exchanger). As the water is heated, it rises out of the cylinder and on to supply the taps.

The other loop supplies the boiler, heat exchanger and—if fitted—the radiators. Here, fresh water flows to the base of the boiler from either the storage tank or from another separate tank, known as the 'expansion tank'.

Once in the boiler, the water is heated and then rises out to feed the heat exchanger and radiators. After the water has given up its heat, it flows back to the boiler to be heated again.

Because the water in this loop is hardly ever changed, the problems of scaling are greatly reduced. The first time it is heated, the water gives up its scale: from then on, it is unable to do further damage.

## The expansion tank
The indirect arrangement works best when an expansion tank is fitted to supply the boiler loop. This makes the loop almost completely independent of the one supplying the hot taps.

The tank is supplied with water from the rising main via another ball-valve. So, if the loop needs topping up with water because of a leak, the process is automatic. In practice, changes in the water level inside the expansion tank are barely noticeable.

# When a pipe bursts

If you are unlucky enough to have a leak or a burst pipe, your first step must be to cut off the water supply. Do this as near to the offending area as possible so that inconvenience is kept to a minimum.

**Hot water pipe or tap:** Look for a stopcock on the pipe which runs into the base of the hot water cylinder or boiler. Before you turn it, make sure that all heating apparatus is off.

**Cold water pipe or tap:** Trac back along the relevant pipe unt you come to a stopcock. If there ar none between the burst and the col storage tank, you will have to bloc the tank outlet. To do this, nail cork slightly larger than the outle hole on to the end of a piece ⬤ timber (fig C). By 'remote control you can now insert the cork int the outlet and prevent furthe water from leaving the tank.

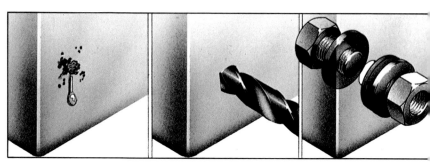

**A.** *A leak in the tank can often be fixed by plugging the hole with a* bolt. *Use a soft washer between th two metal rings for a watertight fit*

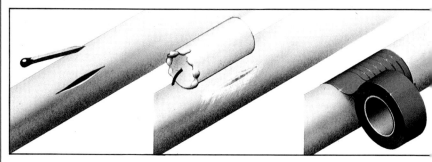

**B.** *Temporary repairs can be made to a split lead pipe by plugging* the crack with a sliver of matchsti waxing the plug, then taping firml

To guard against the build-up of high pressures in the hot water system, overflows or vents are fitted.

In a direct system, only one pipe is needed. This runs to the top of the cold storage tank, either from the crown of the hot water cylinder or from a branch off the hot water service pipe.

In an indirect system, an additional vent is installed at the top point of the primary circuit.

## Turning off the hot water
Whatever your hot water system, the hot water which reaches the taps comes from the top of your hot water cylinder. It does so because of the pressure of the cold water entering

the cylinder beneath.

So, if you cut off the cold wat supply at the base of the cylinder, further hot water will rise from t top. Most hot water cylinders have stopcock for this purpose, fitted at t cold water inlet. Those that do n invariably have a stopcock somewhe on the pipe between the inlet and t cold storage tank. Before touchi this stopcock make sure that all hea ing apparatus is turned off.

## Wet central heating
Wet central heating, in which h water is used to heat the house via system of radiators, adds an additio complication to plumbing instal

Should the outlet prove impossible to block, drain the tank instead. First tie back the ball valve [t]o a piece of timber stretched across [th]e tank (fig.C): this will stop fresh [wa]ter from entering. Now, turn on [yo]ur bath, or washhand basin cold [ta]p, until the tank is fully drained.

**[Ki]tchen cold tap:**
[Tu]rn off the house
[(ri]sing main) stopcock.

**In the garden:** If possible, turn off the water authority stopcock.
**Leaking galvanized storage tank:** A leak here will probably be due to a rust spot which has eaten its way right through the metal. Once you have drained the tank and tied back the ball valve, you can

cure the leak by drilling out the rust spot and fitting a nut and bolt into the hole (fig A).
**Burst lead pipe:** A crack in a lead pipe can be temporarily stopped by ramming in a matchstick and then rubbing the area with candle wax. Follow this by binding up the repair with strong tape (fig B) and keeping any relevant stopcocks at half pressure until a proper repair can be done.

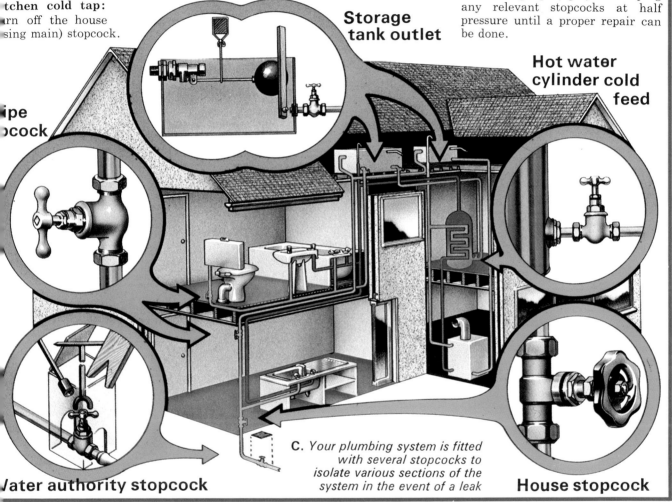

**Storage tank outlet**

**Hot water cylinder cold feed**

**[P]ipe [st]opcock**

**[W]ater authority stopcock**

*C. Your plumbing system is fitted with several stopcocks to isolate various sections of the system in the event of a leak*

**House stopcock**

John Harwood

[reaso]ns. But if you can imagine the radia[to]rs and their pipes as being part of [th]e boiler 'loop' in a basic hot water [sy]stem, the whole thing becomes [ea]sier to understand.
[ ] Some older installations work on [th]e direct principle in which hot [wa]ter heated by the boiler flows to the [ra]diators as well as to the hot taps. [Be]cause this system is uneconomical [an]d causes scaling, it has been [re]placed by indirect installations. [ ] Here, the water which flows to the [ra]diators is on a pump-driven loop like [th]e one used to supply the heat ex[ch]anger. Consequently, it is always [fa]irly hot and requires less heating, [wh]ich in turn makes it far more

economical than a direct system.
In some indirect systems, the water which supplies the boiler loop is drawn direct from the storage tank. But most incorporate a separate expansion tank to keep the loop independent of the rest of the water supply.

## Radiator systems
The pipework used to supply the radiators may take one of two forms. In the simpler, one-pipe system, hot water flows from the boiler to each radiator in turn and then back to the boiler again. Although this cuts down the amount of pipework needed, it allows hot and cooled water to mix near the end of the run. Consequently, the last

radiator in the run often remains cool however hard the boiler is working.
In the two-pipe system, the pipework is arranged so that cooled water leaving the radiators cannot mix with the hot water entering them. The radiators therefore heat up faster, as well as remaining at the same temperature.
Sizing of inward and outward piping in the radiator circuit is matched to the given radiator load. At the boiler a 28mm width supply pipe may be used, this reducing to 22mm at the branch-off point of each radiator bank. Tubing 15mm in diameter is then used to connect the first radiator, and to continue the supply run in the case of a two-pipe system.

# Decorating with tiles

● **Estimating quantities** ● **Types of tile** ●
**Preparing the surface** ● **Getting the tiles square**
● **Cutting and shaping tiles** ● **Tiling around
windows** ● **Tiling in awkward places**

As coverings for walls, tables and working surfaces, ceramic tiles have several distinct advantages over other materials. As well as offering a superb range of colours, patterns and glaze finishes, they make a hard-wearing easy to clean, practical surface.

They also have a high resistance to both acids and alkalis and a permanent colouring, unaffected by prolonged exposure to sunlight or steam.

The one drawback to ceramic tiles is that they are brittle, making them slightly more difficult to work with than vinyl or cork.

### Types of tile
Ceramic tiles come in a wide range of plain colours, patterns and shapes. The three most common sizes are 108mm square x 4mm, 152mm square x 6mm and 152mm x 76mm x 6mm but other sizes are available to order. Australian sizes are 100mm square, 150mm square and 200mm x 100mm. Mosaic tiles—group arrangements of small tiles on backing sheets—are among the other types available.

The field tile used for most tiling usually has lugs around the edges which butt against adjacent tiles and ensure an equal 2mm gap all round.

For edging and corner work, special tiles are available with either one or two rounded edges (fig. A). Border tiles, with two square, glazed edges can be used as an alternative.

Floor tiles are different in strength and suitability to ordinary wall tiles, so check with the supplier before use.

When tiling food preparation surfaces in the kitchen, you should always check with the manufacturer or retailer that the tiles are suitable for the purpose—some have a potentially toxic heavy lead glaze. Tiles used near heat sources such as cookers and fireplaces should be heat resistant or at least 9.5mm thick.

### The basic tool kit
Cutting tools, adhesive and grout readily available from any DIY sho

You will need a simple wheel cut or a scriber with a tungsten-carb tip. A wheel cutter with breaker win for scoring and breaking in c action, costs a little more. A car rundum file is useful for smoothi down the edges of cut tiles.

### Materials
Tile adhesive is available either powder form, to which water is add or else ready-prepared in cans: f litres will cover about 6m² on a gc surface.

However, use a water resistant hesive for areas around sinks, bat and showers and one which is he resistant where temperatures are lil ly to be high, such as around cook and fires.

Grout is a cement-based paste whi is rubbed into the gaps between ti to provide a neat finish. As a rou guide 500g of the powder, mixed w water to a fairly stiff consistency, w

---

## How many tiles?

To estimate how many tiles you will need for a wall or worksurface, measure the length and height in metres then use our formula

**108mm square tiles: Length x Height x 86** = No. of tiles
**152mm square tiles: Length x Height x 43** = No. of tiles
**152mm x 76mm tiles: Length x Height x 86** = No. of tiles

If necessary, add on the required number of special border tiles or subtract tiles to allow for fittings. Add on an extra 5 or 6 tiles to cover breakages.

---

*Cutting tiles is not as hard as it seems. To make a straight cut, simply score a line then snap the tile over a matchstick*

Gavin Cochrane

...ut about 2m² of small tiles or 4m² ...larger ones.

...A non-toxic grout should always be ...d on tiled food preparation surfaces ...d a water resistant grout around ...ks, baths and showers.

## ...eparing the surface

...e quality of any tiling job is largely ...endent on the surface to which the ...s are fixed. This should be firm, ...el, clean and dry with unwanted ...ures such as hooks and screws re- ...ved beforehand.

...Most surfaces require only a little ...paration before they are tiled. A ..., though, need more extensive ...atment: in such cases, think care- ...y before you commit yourself to ...amic tiles.

...ster: Minor bumps and cracks can ...filled with a proprietary plaster ...er. The entire surface should then ...given a coat of plaster primer, to ...vide a non-porous base for the ...hesive. If the surface is very un- ...n, it should be replastered and left ...a month before being sealed and ...d.

...However, rough surfaces can often ...relined with plywood, chipboard or ...sterboard. To do this, you will need ...plug and screw wood battens— ...mm x 25mm will do—to the wall at ...ular intervals. Make sure that ...h batten is vertical, using wood ...ps to pack any gaps between the ...od and the old wall surface.

...Before screwing your panelling ma- ...ial to the battens, give each strip ...horough coat of wood sealant. As ...u secure the panels, plan your work ...that adjacent ones butt up against ...h other over the centre of a batten.

...allpaper: On no account should ...es be laid on to wallpaper. Strip ...wall back to the bare plaster, then ...and level as described above.

...inted walls: Providing these are ...ooth and firm, tiles may be applied ...ect. But flaking or rough paint ...ould be partially stripped with ...dium glasspaper and brushed clean. ...mber walls: These must be sanded ...planed level and treated with wood ...mer before the tiles are applied. ...isting ceramic tiles: The ideal ...ng surface, providing the tiles are ...an, firmly fixed and not chipped.

## ...nstructing a baseline

...fore you start tiling you will need ...horizontal baseline from which to ...rk—floors and skirting boards are ...t suitable, as they are seldom com- ...tely level and can throw the tiling ...t of true.

**1** Make a pencil mark a tile's height from the top edge of the skirting board. This will show you where to draw the baseline

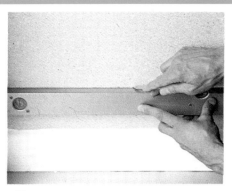

**2** Drawing the baseline. The spirit level ensures that the baseline is level and acts as a straight edge for marking the line

**3** Pin the batten along the bottom of the line to provide a level base for tiling. The bottom row will be filled in later

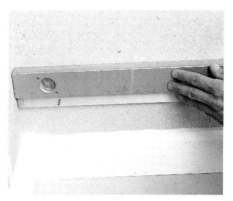

**4** Check the batten with the spirit level to make sure it is horizontal. If it is not, it will have to be unpinned and re-adjusted

**5** Mark tile widths along the batten to give an even cut at each end of the wall. This ensures the symmetry of the tiled wall

**6** Use the spirit level to draw the vertical line at the last tile mark. The line acts as a guide to keep the tiling square

To draw a baseline, measure the height of a tile from the floor or skirting board and make a mark (fig. 1). Using the spirit level as a straight edge, check for level and draw a line through this mark (fig. 2).

Finally, pin the top edge of a batten along the line so it forms a level base, right along the length of the surface to be tiled (fig. 3).

Late, when you have tiled above it, you can remove the batten and fill in the space below (fig. 9). The tiles here may have to be cut or trimmed.

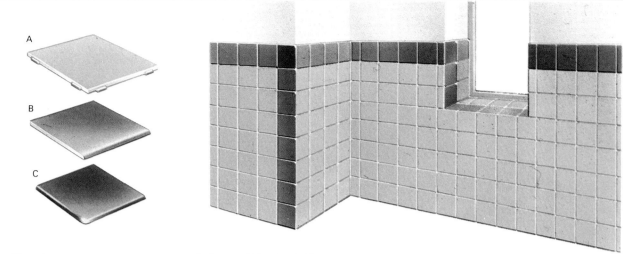

**A**. *The three most common types of tile are* (A) *Field tile* (B) *Single round-edged tile* (C) *Double round-edged tile. The colour coded illustration shows where each type is used*

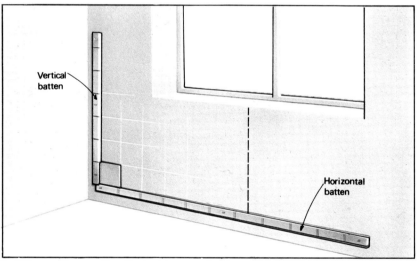

Vertical batten

Horizontal batten

**B**. *When tiling walls, tile inside your horizontal and vertical batten or plumbline first, then remove them and fill in the rest of the space.*

## Tiling around windows

Arrange the tiles to achieve a good visual balance with cut tiles of equal size on each side of the window. When tiling recessed window sills, fit any cut tiles at the back and in the corners where they are not so obvious. Make sure that patterns are kept continuous, and finished surfaces smooth, by placing the spacer lugs of any cut tile against those of the adjacent tile.

Use round-edged tiles at the front of sills, lapping them over the edges of the wall tiles to form a smooth, rounded edge.

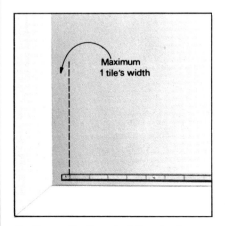

Maximum 1 tile's width

**C**. *Normally the start line is drawn one tile's width away from the edge of the wall with a plumbline*

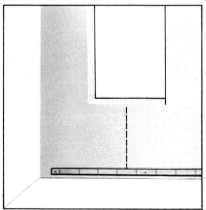

**D**. *When tiling around a window, work from a line down the centre of it—not the edge of the wall*

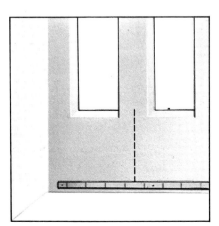

**E**. *On a wall with two windows, the line you work from should run midway between the two*

## arking a side line

keep the tiles exactly square to
baseline, you will also need a
rtical line at one side of the surface.
d the centre point of the batten
d mark out the tile widths along
her end of the wall. Draw your line
ere the last full tile ends on the
thand side, using the spirit level—
a plumb line—to give you an
curate vertical line (fig.6).

## xing the tiles

gin tiling at the intersection of the
izontal batten and the vertical line
.7), filling in the bottom row and
rking upwards.

dhesive should be applied thinly to
wall over an area of not more than
² at a time. If applied to the backs
the tiles themselves, the finished
face could be uneven. If adhesive is
lied over a greater area, some may
before it has been tiled over. Drive
serrated edge of the spreader over
adhesive, forming ridges to pro-
e good suction and adhesion.

**F.** *Mark cutting lines on tiles in felt-tip pen—offering them up to the space they are to fill*

Press the tiles firmly into place
without sliding them, wiping away
any adhesive which squeezes onto the
surface of the tiles with a damp cloth.
The alignment of the tiles should be
checked with the spirit level on com-
pletion of every three or four rows.

When the tiles have set, the corner
tiles may be fixed and the batten removed before filling in the bottom row
—butter their backs with adhesive and
fit them firmly home. Always fit cut
tiles so that the spacer lugs—that is
the uncut sides—faces those of the
adjacent tile (fig.9). For tiles without
lugs, use matchsticks as markers between tiles to ensure even spacing.

Butt the spacer lugs of the tiles on
the adjacent wall against the surface
of the cut corner tile at right angles
to it—thus allowing a grout line to
run down the junction of the two
walls. If the tile has no lugs, space it
with matchsticks.

### Cutting and shaping tiles

Straight cuts in ceramic tiles can be
made either by scoring and snapping
with a standard tile cutter (figs.10 and
11) or by scoring and breaking with
an Oporto tile cutter (fig.12).

Start off by offering the tile to be
cut up to the space on the wall,
positioning it so that it overlaps the

*Fix the first tile at the intersection of the batten and vertical line. Tiles should be ssed firmly home without sliding*

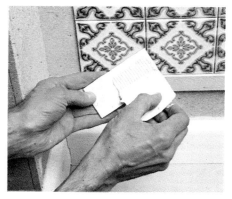

**8** *When fitting cut tiles into corners and awkward areas, adhesive should be applied to the backs of tiles rather than to the wall*

**9** *When the rest of the wall has been tiled, the batten can be removed and the bottom row of tiles cut and fitted into place*

*Use a tile cutter to score through the glazed surface of le. The try square ensures that the re mark is straight and even*

**11** *Place a matchstick under the score mark on the tile. Exert downward pressure and the tile should snap cleanly along the mark*

**12** *An alternative method of cutting tiles is with the Oporto cutter. The tile is snapped by breaker wings.*

adjacent, fixed tile. Mark off the overlap on the tile with felt-tip pen, on the reverse side first, then the glazed side, then the edges.

With the tile back on the bench, convert these marks to a continuous cutting line. Score this line, using a try square to guide you, then either cut the tile with the Oporto cutter or snap it on the bench, over a matchstick.

Notches and curved cuts must be 'nibbled' by hand with a pair of pincers (fig.13). In the case of curved cuts, make a straight cut first as near to the curve as possible—the tile will snap if you attempt to pincer out larger areas.

The guidelines for curved cuts can be drawn in either by eye, or—more satisfactorily—with a cardboard template. Trim the template to shape in situ then transfer it to the tile and draw around it in felt-tip pen.

Pipes present some of the trickiest tiling problems. The safest way to tile around them is to cut the relevant tile in two and to cut a semi-circle out of each half.

All cuts in ceramic tiles look neater and more professional if they are smoothed afterwards with a carborundum file or block (fig 14).

## Tiling around fitments

Where the fitment runs the length of a wall—a bath or kitchen unit for example—treat the top edge as you would a floor or skirting board. Fix a horizontal batten along this edge and leave it in place while you tile the wall above. When the tiles are dry, remove the batten and tile down to the edge with tiles cut to fit.

Where the fitment is in the middle of a wall—such as a basin or wc—tile around it as closely as you can with whole tiles, then fill in the spaces with cut tiles when the rest of the wall is completed.

## Grouting

When the tiling is finished, leave it to set for 12 to 24 hours, then rub grout firmly into the tile joints with an old sponge, squeegee or cloth (fig.15). Remove excess grout with a damp sponge: when it has almost set, run a blunt stick across the joints to leave a neat finish (fig.16). Allow the grout to dry and then give the tiles a final polish with a soft, dry cloth.

**13** *For a shaped cut, score the area that is to be removed then nibble out small pieces of the tile with a pair of pincers*

**14** *When the shape has been nibbled out of the tile, smooth off any unevenness on the cut edge with a carborundum file*

**15** *Once the tiling has been completed and the adhesive has set, rub grout firmly into the joints with a sponge or piece of rag*

**16** *When the grout is almost dry draw a stick with a round point along the joints to give a neat appearance to the finished tiling*

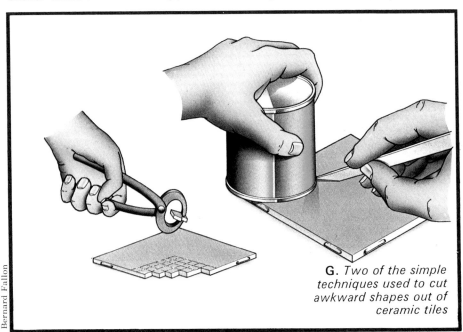

**G.** *Two of the simple techniques used to cut awkward shapes out of ceramic tiles*

Bernard Fallon

# Stylish tiled worktop

You can brighten up that old shabby work top in the kitchen simply and inexpensively by tiling over the existing surface and smartening up the space below the cupboards with shelves and cork tiles on the wall.

A couple of strip lights installed behind the cupboard overhang provide a good working light across the tiled surface and concentrate light where it is most needed, making the work surface free from shadows.

Be sure to use unglazed tiles as constant use will destroy the surface of the glazed variety. Take care, too, to use a non-toxic grout.

Follow the designs overleaf for the basic construction details plus hints on how to build-in a knife rack and chopping board as part of the worktop.

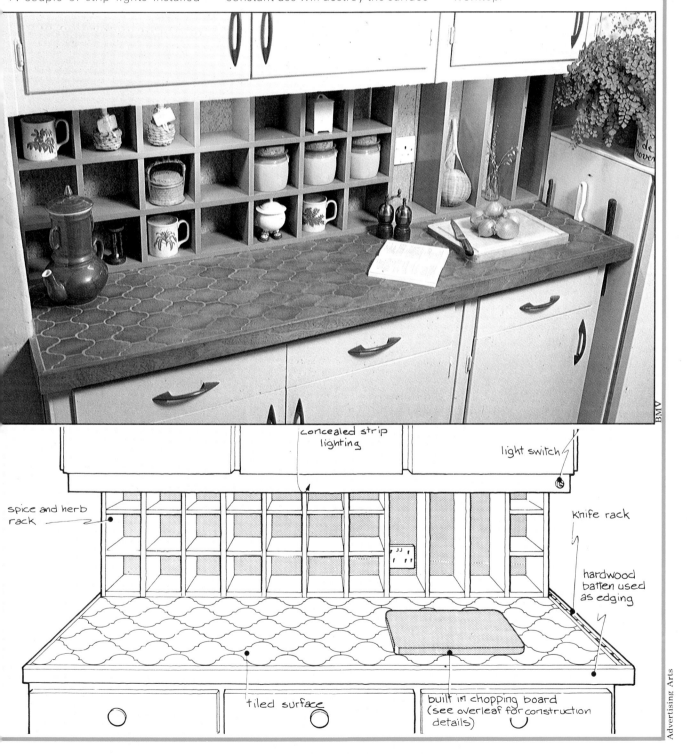

concealed strip lighting

light switch

spice and herb rack

knife rack

hardwood batten used as edging

tiled surface

built in chopping board (see overleaf for construction details)

BMV

Advertising Arts

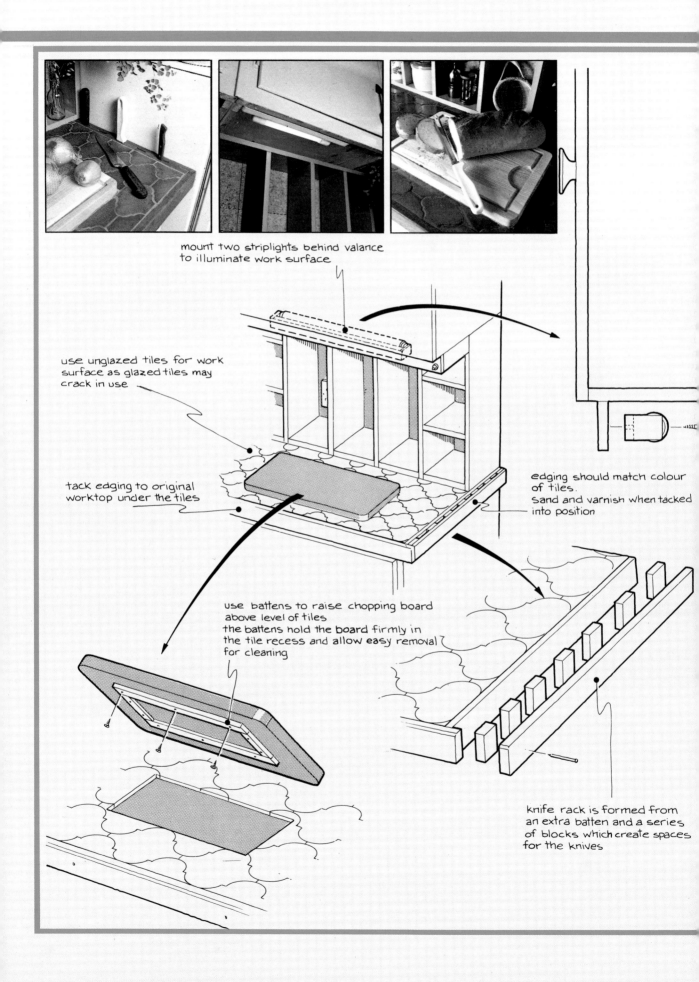

mount two striplights behind valance
to illuminate work surface

use unglazed tiles for work
surface as glazed tiles may
crack in use

tack edging to original
worktop under the tiles

edging should match colour
of tiles.
sand and varnish when tacked
into position

use battens to raise chopping board
above level of tiles
the battens hold the board firmly in
the tile recess and allow easy removal
for cleaning

knife rack is formed from
an extra batten and a series
of blocks which create spaces
for the knives

# Make the most of your windows

**A well-dressed window provides a natural focus of attention. Imaginative use of curtains, blinds, shutters or screens can completely transform any room**

The need for privacy may be an important factor in choosing your window dressings for the living room. Although curtains are the obvious choice, they are by no means the only one—blinds, sheers and screens can be just as versatile and are often more economical where there is a large window area to cover.

In a room which is overlooked, a permanent screen of some kind—combined with curtains—is the best solution. Fixed sheers are a very popular solution, but you could use mirrored glass or even a solar reflective panel. The latter allows you to look out of the window while leaving passers-by with just a reflection of themselves.

An inexpensive way to make an attractive free-standing screen is to use a section of wooden garden trellis, painted to match the existing decor. This lets in a fair amount of light, at the same time masking an unsightly view and giving you privacy.

Another suggestion which works for a sash window is to hang a wooden blind (pinoleum type) over the bottom part, with a roller blind at the top.

Where privacy is not a consideration and you want to make the most of a view, Roman blinds may be the answer. Raised and lowered by a series of cords which fold them up into concertina-like pleats, they are highly versatile. When fully raised they look similar to a valance; when lowered the pleats even out and the blind lays flat against the window.

On a large expanse of glass—such as a picture window—use two or three Roman blinds of equal width rather than a single one, which might be difficult to handle.

Roman blinds can be given a subtle sophistication with a matching pelmet and a fixed sheer screen. The sheer looks best if it complements the blind fabric—some sheers have such lovely designs that they should only be stretched flat against the window.

Almost any kind of window treatment will work in the living room—it all depends on the sort of effect you are looking for. Choose the fabric carefully as this considerably affects the overall feel of the dressing. A velvet and, say, a candy-striped fabric can be hung exactly the same way, but the looks you achieve with them will be entirely different.

Use roller blinds if your taste is for

**Below:** *Screens are an unusual way to disguise windows. They can easily be folded back when not in use*

# Home designer

big and bold patterns—these fabrics look much more effective when the design is not distorted by the pleated effect of curtaining. And if you cannot decide whether you want full-length curtains or blinds, use both. This combination is ideal when there is a radiator immediately under the window. With the blind down and curtains open, the draughts are kept out and the heat kept in.

Roller blinds are often hung inside the window reveal, exposing the bare surround and frame. If you dislike this, either team the blinds with complementary curtains, or outline the surround with a thin painted line of a contrasting colour. This creates a very attractive 'framing' effect around the blind.

Pinoleum blinds, which are made from very fine strips of wood sewn together with cotton are becoming popular for living rooms. They usually come in natural pine or stained green and blend particularly well into a modern or farmhouse look. Reasonably priced, they make an economical dressing for a large living room window. When fully let down, they allow a gentle amount of light to filter through.

## Dining room/study

Whether the decor you have chosen gives this room a sophisticated or a practical atmosphere, eating or studying should be a comfortable activity. So, it is best to avoid anything too dramatic in the window treatment.

Shutters are a good, unobtrusive way of providing light and privacy control and make an attractive change from more conventional approaches. If the window is a wide one, it could take an open-weave bamboo type which opens and closes horizontally like a concertina.

Most of the shutters available are louvred but remember, the louvres

**Above**: *Pinoleum blinds add a sophisticated touch to any room letting in plenty of light but still maintaining privacy.* **Left**: *Roman blinds are versatile, stylish and suit any window*
**Below**: *No-nonsense shutters are ideal for the study or dining room where a straightforward window dressing is required.* **Opposite**: *Not all shutters are plain and simple. This set of multiple shutters can be arranged to suit any mood by adjusting the concertina folds*

National Magazine Co.

Elizabeth Whiting

National Magazine Co.

window dressings for the simpler kind of bedroom. If you mount a blind upside down you can have it half closed to cover just the lower part of the window, giving you privacy and a fair amount of light at the same time. The pullcord can be extended and run from the top of the window frame to a small ceiling pulley and then on to a cleat near the bedside, so you can even operate the blinds from the bed.

Blinds in bright, simple colours look good for a child's room, or for an adult bedroom with clean, modern lines. But, if you prefer something less stark, you can achieve a softer look by combining curtains or scalloped pelmets in the same material.

## Bathroom

Most bathroom windows are frosted or dimpled in some way to give the room privacy. This is fine if the view outside is boring but not so good if you have a pretty and private outlook. If you want the view as well as your privacy, consider covering just the lower part of the window and leaving the upper part plain glass.

For instance fit mirrored glass to the lower part—and you have a vanity mirror and room-enlarger as well as a screen. Or fit a cafe-style curtain—hanging on a pole mid-way down the window—using heavy fabric or plastic which resists the bathroom steam.

Plants thrive in the steamy atmosphere of a bathroom and can be used to good effect as window decorations —either hung in the window in large

not always have to be fixed ver-
lly. Wide windows or very tall
dows look most attractive when
ir shape is broken up with alternate
cks of both horizontal and vertical
vred shutters.

enetian blinds are ideal for rooms
ere softness is not the main con-
eration. They have moved on from
clinical white in which they first
eared and now come in many
ractive colours to blend with most
ur schemes. Their clean and
ple appearance makes them es-
ially suited to a study where you
nt as little distraction as possible.
uched blinds make an attractive
ion for the dining room—if the
terial is not too fussy. They have
athered look even when let down
work very well in small rooms
ere full-length curtains would look
mped or overbearing.

### droom

en choosing window dressings for
bedroom, you should consider
ether you want complete privacy—
h every scrap of dawn light kept
—or bright, airy surroundings.
ide, too, whether the overall effect
o be exotic, simple or romantic.
urtains are the most effective way
shutting out light completely.
oose the double-tracked kind—
h netting or a sheer on the inner
ck. These are curved so there is
gap at the top of the window.
uched curtains in delicate pastel
des and flimsy fabrics soften any
pe of window and give the bedroom
omantic look. You can accentuate

this effect by teaming them with 'dummy' curtains tied back at the sides of the window.

If you have a large enough window and want to go one step further with your curtain dressing, top the window with a valance. These look especially pretty when gathered into a series of pleats and neatly complement the dummy side curtains. For a totally co-ordinated look, you can match the bed linen and accessories to your window dressing fabric.

Fabric roller blinds make attractive

Bill McLaughlin

baskets or arranged on rows of flo
glass shelves set across the windo
Depending on the number of pla
and shelves used, this type of dress
can give you a lot of privacy, yet s
let the light in.

Translucent sheer fabrics are a
other way to achieve this effe
Sheers look their best gathered
and bottom on to poles fitted in
window reveal. This lets through
shimmering light while maintain
a fair degree of privacy.

If you want something really ha
wearing and splash-resistant, ro
blinds in PVC or oilskin are ideal.

## Kitchen

Although you need to choose so
thing very practical for a kitch
window, there is still lots of sc
for introducing attractive colours a
patterns. Some of the more specta
lar roller blinds, for example, ha
complete scenes hand-painted
printed on them—the ideal solut
to basement kitchen windows wh
offer nothing but a brick wall fo
view.

**Left**: *Co-ordinated wallpaper and
curtains liven up what could easily
have been a dull, lifeless window*
**Below**: *A stretched sheer mask
ensures privacy and provides a
pretty contrast to the curtains*

Marshall Cavendish

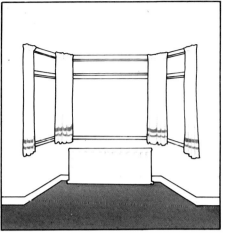

...rack with full-length curtains fitted ...ross the outer reveal of a bay ...ndow adds depth to its attractive ...ape without blocking out any light

With this arrangement of four sill-length curtains, neither the bay area nor the heat from the radiator is lost at night when the curtains are drawn

Recessed windows are best fitted with a curved track so that the curtains can be pulled back to allow in the greatest amount of light

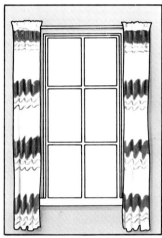

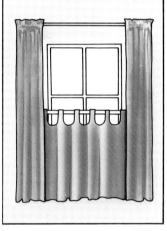

...l, thin windows lose less of their light-giving potential ...d look much wider if the curtain track and curtains are ...ended beyond the reveal. Horizontal patterns on the ...tains enhance the widening effect

A more interesting appearance can be given to small, square windows firstly by raising the curtain track and lengthening the curtains. And secondly by adding a cafe curtain which conceals the window ledge

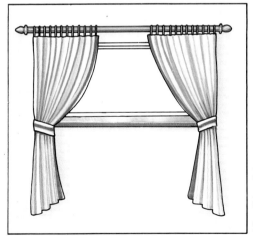

...o odd-shaped windows sited side-by-side look more of a pair if they ...given the same window treatment. Here, the curtain track has been ...d above the smaller window frame and the curtains extended beyond ...sill to bring it in line with the other, larger window

Plain, horizontal windows can take a lot of dressing up—such as decorative curtain rods and tie-backs. A vertical pattern and extended length adds depth

Advertising Arts

Available ready-made in bright colours, vinyl blinds are hardwearing and need only a wipe-down with a damp cloth to keep them sparkling clean. Fabric blinds are slightly less practical but often more attractive. If you plan to make your own blind using a kit choose either a PVC or tightly woven cotton or linen fabric, which rolls evenly without sagging.

If the window is located above the sink—making it relatively inaccessible—a roller blind cord may be difficult to reach. In this case, a vertical louvre blind—a more recent variation of the venetian blind—is the answer. They have a side opening and closing system which can be reached without stretching. Vertical louvre blinds also let in more light than roller blinds.

If curtains are feasible, you might consider cotton gingham—an old favourite for kitchens, this fabric is never really out of fashion.

## Landing or stairway

Windows which are located half-way up or at the top of stairs, generally do not need to be screened from passers-by. They can be given a treatment which is decorative but which does not actually cover the window.

For something different, try using stencils and transparent glass paints to make a pretty design on the window. Or, brightly-coloured and varnished wooden beads threaded on strings and glued to a length of dowelling could be fitted to the top of the window.

**Below**: *A vinyl roller blind is the most sensible solution for a bathroom window. A quick wipe with a damp cloth and splash marks disappear*

Michael Boys/Susan Griggs

# A simple Roman blind

Roman blinds are the simplest ki of window dressing and you c make your own far cheaper th the shop bought variety.

To make the blind shown opp site you will need a suitable leng of material to fit your chosen w dow. Buy material to allow fo side hem wide enough and b enough length for a loop to made at the bottom in which to the batten.

You will need four pulley brack —obtainable from your hardwa store and a suitable length nylon draw cord.

The fabric should be fairly flexi so that it hangs properly in fo when the blind is drawn up.

Buy material with a fairly ge metric design as this looks p ticularly good when folded back itself, the bold shapes stacki under each other for maxim visual impact.

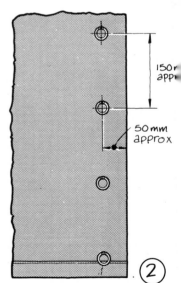

150 r
appr

50 mm
approx

② 

sew 4 sets of rings to the reverse side of the blind. space rings equally apart with the two outer rows approx 50 mm from edges

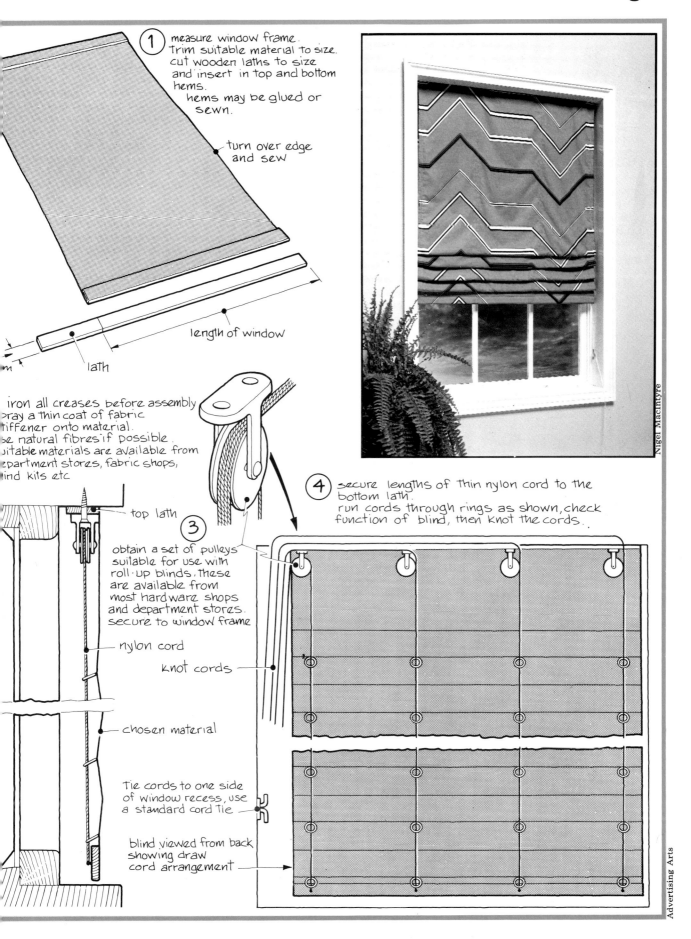

1. measure window frame. Trim suitable material to size. cut wooden laths to size and insert in top and bottom hems. hems may be glued or sewn.

turn over edge and sew

length of window

lath

iron all creases before assembly
pray a thin coat of fabric
tiffener onto material.
e natural fibres if possible.
uitable materials are available from
epartment stores, fabric shops,
ind kits etc

top lath

3. obtain a set of pulleys suitable for use with roll·up blinds. these are available from most hardware shops and department stores. secure to window frame

nylon cord

knot cords

chosen material

Tie cords to one side of window recess, use a standard cord Tie

blind viewed from back showing draw cord arrangement

4. secure lengths of thin nylon cord to the bottom lath. run cords through rings as shown, check function of blind, then knot the cords.

Nigel MacIntyre

Advertising Arts

43

# Squaring up, sawing and sanding

- **Types of saw** ● **Measuring and marking up timber** ● **Scribing with a marking gauge** ● **Measuring and marking** ● **Starting a saw cut** ● **Sawing techniques** ● **Hand-sanding**

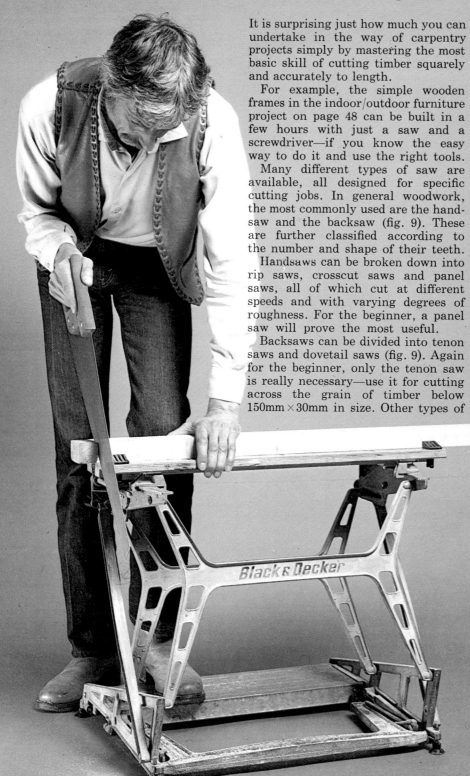

It is surprising just how much you can undertake in the way of carpentry projects simply by mastering the most basic skill of cutting timber squarely and accurately to length.

For example, the simple wooden frames in the indoor/outdoor furniture project on page 48 can be built in a few hours with just a saw and a screwdriver—if you know the easy way to do it and use the right tools.

Many different types of saw are available, all designed for specific cutting jobs. In general woodwork, the most commonly used are the hand-saw and the backsaw (fig. 9). These are further classified according to the number and shape of their teeth.

Handsaws can be broken down into rip saws, crosscut saws and panel saws, all of which cut at different speeds and with varying degrees of roughness. For the beginner, a panel saw will prove the most useful.

Backsaws can be divided into tenon saws and dovetail saws (fig. 9). Again for the beginner, only the tenon saw is really necessary—use it for cutting across the grain of timber below 150mm × 30mm in size. Other types of saw—such as the coping saw a padsaw—are used for more speciali: cutting work: they are describ further on in the course.

A solid working surface is essent for quick and accurate saw cutti If you do not already have a w bench of some sort, an old ta covered in 6mm hardboard and u in conjunction with a home-ma bench hook (figs 11 and 12) sho see you through most cutting jobs.

For detailed work at a later sta you may need to add a vice to bench. Alternatively, you could inv in a collapsible work bench wh serves as a work surface, large v and drilling rig all in one. Makin purpose-built work bench is cove further on in the course.

## Measuring and marking up

Any slight errors made in measuri and marking will multiply when y come to start sawing and may ru your project. The best way to avoi mistake is to check every measu ment twice.

Having selected the piece of timb to be worked on—the workpiece inspect it carefully. With a try squa determine which is the straighte adjacent side and edge and mark th in pencil (figs 1 and 2). Always wc from these when using any measuri or marking tool—this will ensure th the marks are consistent. A try squa is an essential marking tool and co very little.

For measuring, use a steel rule boxwood rule where possible: you m need a steel tape on longer pieces timber or boards, but this is not accurate.

Mark out distances in pencil, usi a 'vee' mark as shown in fig. 2 this tells you exactly where you ha measured to and is another tip avoiding errors. Where possible, c out marks altogether by using t try square and rule as shown in fig.

Where accuracy is essential, ma cutting lines with a sharp knife preferably a marking knife—not w a pencil. The scored line made by

**A.** *The correct position for sawing across a piece of timber with a pane or crosscut handsaw. Movement of t sawing arm is unobstructed, the sav is held at about 45° and the head is looking straight down over the blad*

44

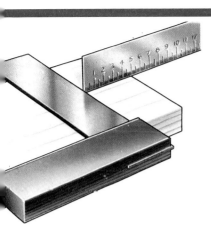

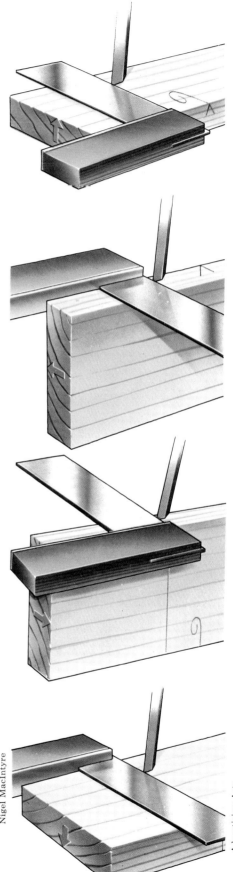

**B.** *Left: Where possible, measure timber with just a rule and a try square. This saves time and is more accurate than lining the square up with pencil marks*

**C.** *Right: When scribing cutting lines around a piece of timber, it is most important to do so in the correct order and with the try square in the right place. After scribing a mark, turn the timber in the direction of the red arrow and line your try square with the 'nick' left by it to continue the line around*

...ife is thinner, and therefore more ...curate, than a pencil line. Also, it ...ves to break the outer fibres of the ...ber, thereby stopping the saw cut ...m fraying.

...s you scribe a cutting line, use ... try square to guide you (fig. 3). ...ur free hand should control the ... square without obstructing the ...rking knife. Keep the stock of the ... square flush against the face or ...ge of the workpiece, with the blade ...t on the surface you are marking. ...e edge of the blade should line up ...actly with the points of the vee ...ncil marks.

...When making a straight, 90 degree ...t across a piece of timber, mark ...t lines all round the workpiece ... shown in fig. C).

**...ribing**

...ribing with a marking gauge (fig. 6) ...en saves a great deal of laborious ...asuring and marking. Marking ...uges are cheap and really make life ...sier when marking out. The tech-...que takes a bit of practice to master, ... you should experiment on wood ...cuts before starting any serious ...ribing work.

...To set the marking gauge to the

required distance—
● Measure off this distance between the sliding block and the needle point (fig. 4).
● Tighten the sliding block so that it just grips the shaft.
● Recheck the measurement against your rule.

If you find that the sliding block moved slightly as you tightened it, make adjustments by gripping the gauge as shown in fig. 5 and tapping it sharply on the bench. Check the measurement after each tap, until it is exactly right.

To scribe a mark, arrange the workpiece with the gauge nearest you. Make sure that the sliding block is flush against your face side or edge, then roll the gauge towards you until the needle touches the wood (fig. 6). Keeping the gauge at this angle, run it away from you down the workpiece to scribe the line. Avoid applying excessive pressure as you do this: if the needle digs in too far, a wavering line will result.

To scribe a line down the middle of a workpiece, set your marking gauge to roughly half its width and make a mark from the face edge. Make a mark from the opposite edge in the

*Slide your try square up and down the workpiece as shown to ...d out which two sides form the ...st perfect right-angle*

**2** *Having decided this, mark the two sides as 'face edge'—with a vee mark—and 'face side'—with an 'f'. Always work from these*

Nigel MacIntyre

Advertising Arts

# Carpentry 1

**3** To scribe a cutting line, hold the try square as shown. If you are working to pencil marks, ensure that you line up the square properly

**4** Set a marking gauge against your rule as shown. When the slide is as near as you can get it, tighten the lock slightly to hold it

**5** Make final adjustments by holding the gauge as shown and tapping it sharply on the bench. Check with the ruler after each tap

**6** To scribe with the gauge, tilt it towards you until the needle just touches the wood then run the gauge away from you down the timber

same way, adjust the gauge, then continue making marks from either edge until the two marks coincide. When they do, you have found the middle and can scribe accordingly from the face side or edge.

## Solving marking problems

Occasionally, you may come across a piece of timber which is difficult to mark up because of its shape and size.

To find the length of a workpiece longer than your rule or tape, measure a certain distance along it from one end then measure the same distance from the other end. Mark both points and measure between them. Add this to your two original measurements to get the overall length.

If you need to find the centre of this piece, simply divide your third measurement by two and mark off.

Dividing a piece of hardboard into equal strips can become extremely confusing unless the overall width divides exactly. Provided that no great accuracy is called for, you can get round the problem by running your tape or rule across one end of the

workpiece and angling it until you get a measurement which is easily divisible by the strips required (fig. 7).

Mark off each division then repeat the process at the other end of the workpiece. Scribe the cutting line for each strip against a rule or straight edge, lined up with these marks (fig. 8). If the board is narrow enough do this with the marking gauge.

**7** Measurements which do not divide exactly can be made divisible by angling your rule. Mark off, then repeat on the other side

Before you start cutting the strips bear in mind that some wood will be lost during the cutting process—using a panel saw, about 1.5mm per cut. This wastage is known as the kerf. For really accurate work, make allowances for it on each strip.

## Sawing timber

The first important rule about sawing timber is that you should always saw on the waste side of the cutting line. Where accuracy is vital—as in furniture or shelf making—this means that you should always allow 5mm 10mm waste wood between one piece of timber and the next. For this type of work never be tempted to economize by simply dividing the timber into the required lengths—inaccuracies creep in, compounding as you work down.

Your sawing position is also crucial: get this right and you are well on the way to getting a perfect cut every time. Fig. A shows the correct stance. Note that you should stand slightly 'sideways on'.

If your timber is at all damp, you can make sawing easier by lightly rubbing over the saw blade with a candle (fig. 10).

## Starting the cut

Make sure that your workpiece is firmly held and will not 'jar' as you saw. If you are using a bench hook, arrange the workpiece so that as much of it as possible is supported on the bench. Use your free hand to press the timber against the raised lip of the bench hook as you saw.

To start the cut, line up your saw blade against the cutting line and rest it against your thumb (fig. 11). Keeping your thumb still and the saw at the optimum angle of 30 to degrees, make a few short strokes towards you until you have grazed

**8** Having marked the divisions, use a rule, straight edge or—where possible—a marking gauge to turn the marks into cutting lines

**1** *A handsaw and two backsaws. From top to bottom: general-purpose panel saw, tenon saw, and dovetail saw—used for intricate work*

**10** *When you are dealing with damp or unseasoned timber, waxing the saw blade first with a candle will make sawing easier*

**11** *Start saw cuts with the blade up against your thumb. Use short, sharp strokes to begin with then lengthen them as the cut grows*

**2** *Using a mitre block. Steady the block as you saw, by holding it against a bench hook or clamping it in a vice*

wood. As you do this, look along the saw blade and keep your face side and face edge cutting lines in view.

As you get into your stroke—that is, start sawing in both directions—try the saw in a 'bowing' motion to keep the cut firmly fixed on both cutting lines. Keep the saw at right-angles to the workpiece, to ensure an accurate cut across the timber.

Well into the cut, lengthen your stroke to make as much use of the saw blade as possible. At the same time, bring down the heel of the saw to ensure that you follow the lines on the two visible surfaces. Use short, sharp strokes to stop the undersurface of the wood from fraying as you finish off the cut.

**Sawing with the grain**

The need to saw a piece of timber lengthways with the grain can usually be avoided, simply by buying the correct-sized timber to start with.

But if long-grain sawing is unavoidable, place the timber or board across two trestles at about knee height. Support the timber with your free

hand and knee. Position your body so as to give free movement to your sawing arm with your body weight balanced over the cut.

Use a cross-cut or panel saw for boards up to 15mm thick and for all man-made boards: use a rip saw on heavier timber.

If the timber begins to pinch the saw blade—causing inaccuracies—open up the kerf with thin wedges.

Although the optimum cutting angle for long grain cuts is normally 45 degrees, cut thin sheet material and plastic-faced boards at 10-15 degrees to the workpiece.

If the saw wanders to one side of the line, gently bend the blade back in the opposite direction until correct cutting line is achieved.

**Making 45 degree cuts**

To make 45 degree cuts quickly and accurately, carpenters use a mitre block (fig. 12) or box. These are available quite cheaply from DIY shops and builders' merchants.

Hold your workpiece firmly against the block as you cut. Rest the block itself against a bench hook or, alternatively, clamp it in a vice.

Always use a backsaw to do the cutting, keeping the blade flatter than usual—although the cut may take longer, you will avoid accidental damage to the box itself.

**Hand-sanding timber**

Nearly all hand-sanding work should be done with a cork sanding block—available cheaply from most DIY shops. You have a wide choice of woodworking abrasive paper—including Garnet paper, Glass paper and Silicon Carbide to name but a few. But each carries a grading number on the back referring to its grit size, which is a guide to its abrasive pro-

perties. Often, there will also be a more general classification—coarse, medium or fine.

Coarse grade paper is too abrasive for most sanding work, so you should rely only on the medium and fine grades. Try out the fine grade paper first and if you find that this works without too much effort, stick to it for the entire job. If you have to use the medium grade paper, remember to finish off with the fine grade.

To economize on abrasive paper, fold each sheet into six, equal-sized rectangles and cut it up. Each rectangle will give you just enough to wrap round the sanding block.

The key to sanding along the length of a piece of timber is to use long, uniform strokes—keeping with the grain at all times. Short strokes tend to create hollows and ridges.

To sand the end grain, use the technique shown in fig. 13. Always start by smoothing down the four edges, keeping your paper flat on the bench. This will stop them from fraying as you block-sand the rest of the grain.

Nigel MacIntyre

**13** *Chamfer the edges of a piece of timber as shown before you sand the end-grain. This will prevent the wood from fraying*

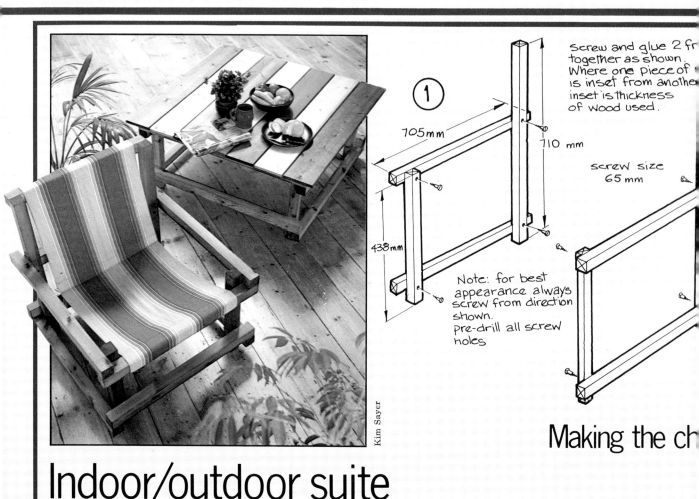

Kim Sayer

Screw and glue 2 fr
together as shown.
Where one piece of
is inset from anothe
inset is thickness
of wood used.

① 705mm  710 mm

438mm

screw size
65 mm

Note: for best
appearance always
screw from direction
shown.
Pre-drill all screw
holes

## Making the ch

# Indoor/outdoor suite

## Cutting list

For each chair, you need lengths of 50mm×50mm softwood in the following sizes: 4 pieces 705mm; 2 pieces 710mm; 5 pieces 700mm; 2 pieces 438mm. You also need 20 64mm×No 10 screws, 12 19mm×No 6 screws and 1600mm of seating material bought to deck-chair width.

The frame of the table also utilizes 50mm×50mm softwood, in the following lengths: 5 pieces ×955mm; 4 pieces ×930mm; 4 pieces 420mm. For the top, you need 7 softwood planks 1016mm ×153mm×19mm. The screws are 25 64mm×No 10 and 50 57mm× No 8.

**Above:** *This indoor/outdoor style furniture is easily built in a day. A variety of finishes can be achieved —the suite above was simply stained with green, then clear, wood preservative to bring out the natural grain pattern*

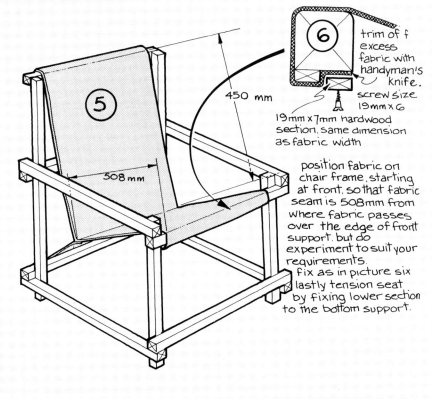

⑥ trim of f
excess
fabric with
handyman's
knife.
screw size
19mm×6

450 mm

⑤ 508mm

19mm×7mm hardwood
section, same dimension
as fabric width

position fabric on
chair frame, starting
at front, so that fabric
seam is 508mm from
where fabric passes
over the edge of front
support, but do
experiment to suit your
requirements.
fix as in picture six
lastly tension seat
by fixing lower section
to the bottom support.

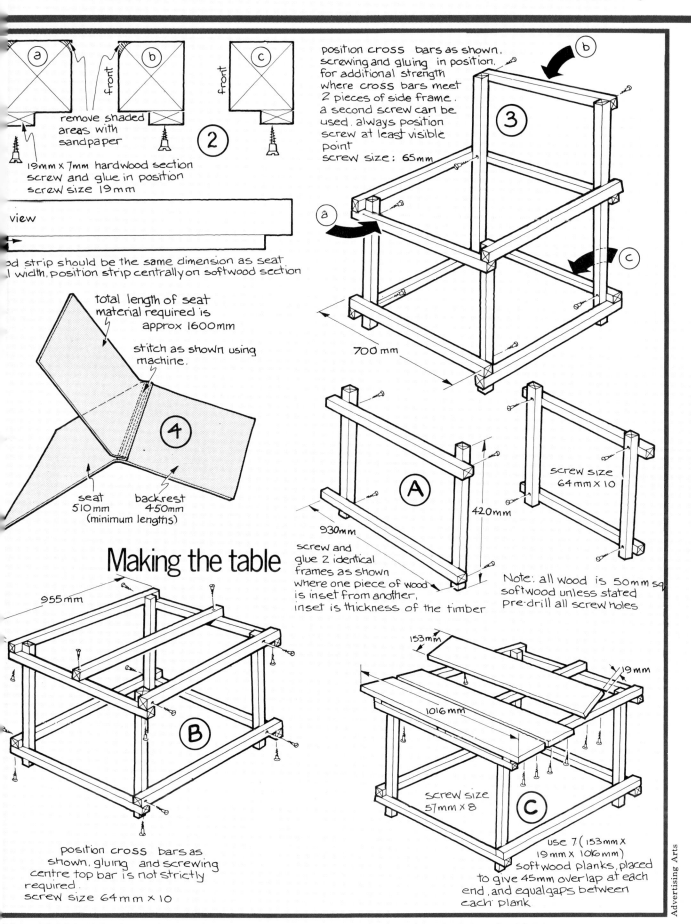

remove shaded
areas with
sandpaper

②

19mm x 7mm hardwood section
screw and glue in position
screw size 19mm

view

od strip should be the same dimension as seat
l width, position strip centrally on softwood section

total length of seat
material required is
approx 1600mm

stitch as shown using
machine.

④

seat          backrest
510mm        450mm
(minimum lengths)

position cross bars as shown.
screwing and gluing in position.
for additional strength
where cross bars meet
2 pieces of side frame.
a second screw can be
used. always position
screw at least visible
point
screw size: 65mm

③

700 mm

Ⓐ

930mm

screw and
glue 2 identical
frames as shown
where one piece of wood
is inset from another,
inset is thickness of the timber

screw size
64mm x 10

420mm

Note: all wood is 50mm sq
softwood unless stated
pre-drill all screw holes

## Making the table

955mm

Ⓑ

position cross bars as
shown. gluing and screwing
centre top bar is not strictly
required.
screw size 64mm x 10

153mm

1016mm

19mm

screw size
57mm x 8

Ⓒ

use 7 (153mm x
19mm x 1016mm)
softwood planks, placed
to give 45mm overlap at each
end, and equal gaps between
each plank

# Working with copper pipe

● **Working with copper piping** ● **Cutting and preparing pipework** ● **Easy connections with a non-manipulative compression joint** ● **Fitting a shower/mixer tap set**

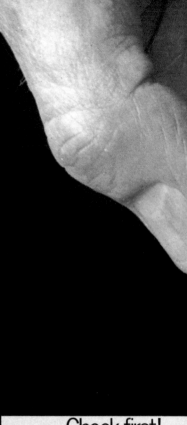

Copper is now the most widely used material for pipework. And unlike the old lead pipes which preceded it, copper pipe is quite easy to work with. Once you know how to cut, bend and join it, a whole host of home improvement projects become possible.

Although expensive, the choice of copper as a piping material is a natural one. It does not rust, it is suitable for both hot and cold water systems and it is soft enough to work with in tight corners. Plastics piping is gaining in popularity but has not, as yet, replaced copper—systems capable of dealing with hot water are a relatively new development.

The sizes of copper pipe used in domestic plumbing have gradually become standardized—typically 22mm for the rising main (see page 27) and for certain low-pressure installations, and 15mm for the pipe used to supply outlets such as sink and basin taps or washing machines. But in older installations, imperial measurements are still found.

Although any new pipe or fitting you buy will be metric, the existing pipe-work to which it is being joined may be in an imperial size—especially in an older house. Joining the two is not difficult, but you must be aware

of the difference and allow for it.

In most instances, incorporation of further copper plumbing within an existing system presents few problems. But if joints have to be made to old lead or iron piping be wary: unless you already have some practical plumbing experience, seek the advice of a plumber (working with lead pipe is covered further on in the course). Normally, this would apply only to those modernizing the plumbing of older houses. Nearly all modern domestic plumbing installations are based on the use of copper, stainless-steel or plastics piping.

## Tools

Few specialist items of equipment are really necessary for the more straightforward plumbing jobs such as cutting pipe and making simple types of join. Most of the items can be found in every handyman's toolbox—you need a good quality hacksaw with medium-fine blade, a flexible steel 2m rule, wrenches, adjustable spanners, files, and steel wool.

It is often possible to get round the need for making your own bends by planning the pipe run in advance and by a careful choice of the available fittings (fig. B).

**1** Carefully unroll a length of tubing from a supply coil, straightening as you go. Wider tubing is available only in pre-cut lengths

Paul Williams

**2** Measure off the required lengths for each section of piping. Cutting marks can be pencilled, or scored with a nail or screwdriver

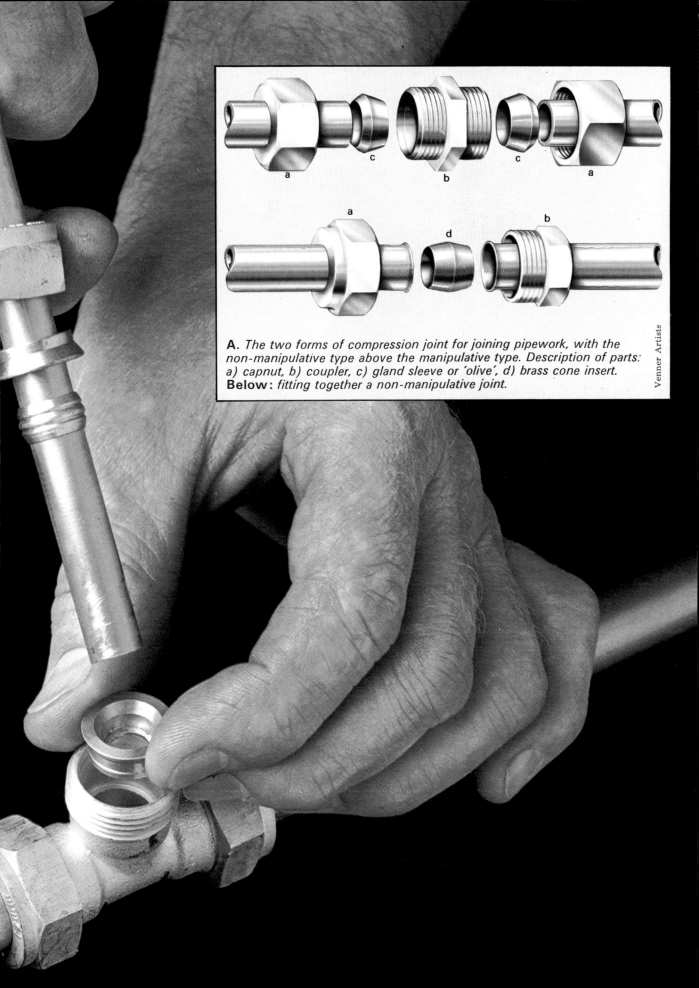

**A.** *The two forms of compression joint for joining pipework, with the non-manipulative type above the manipulative type. Description of parts: a) capnut, b) coupler, c) gland sleeve or 'olive', d) brass cone insert.* **Below:** *fitting together a non-manipulative joint.*

Venner Artists

**3** Use a medium-fine bladed hacksaw to make a clean and square cut, essential for good jointing later on

**4** Larger pieces of swarf are easier removed by knife, but take care to avoid injury as the swarf can be extremely sharp

**5** Hone down the outside edge using a broad-blade flat file, taking care not to distort thin-bore tubing while doing so

**6** Smooth down internal burrs using a round file, and then complete the preparations by cleaning the joint region

Pipe bending is not a particularly difficult skill, but usually requires use of a blowlamp for best results—this is a subject covered in the next stage of the plumbing course. Ready-made bend sections—or fittings—can be used instead but are expensive on all but a short pipe run.

### Measuring and cutting

The first task is to estimate the amount of pipe required for your project. This can be done by using scale plans you have prepared or better, from direct measurement of the run using a flexible steel tape. For really tricky pipe runs, use a piece of wire instead of the tape—feed it along the route first, then measure its length. As purpose-made fittings permit much sharper bends than bend sections consider using these.

### Cutting copper pipe

At its simplest, cutting copper p requires only a straight eye, a grip and a hacksaw. But in order avoid problems later on, you sho make sure that each cut is as cl and as straight as possible. Ta particular care in finishing a cut.

If a great deal of cutting has to done, consider investing in, or hiri a pipe cutter (fig.7). It is recomm ded for use only on the thick walled piping as there is sc tendency for the cutting area to crimped if thin pipe is being cut. T might impede water flow later, res ing in noise-inducing turbulence w in the pipe.

First, using a fine-toothed flat f straighten and smooth out the edge. Any ragged edges that are will probably cause leaks later on,

**7** If you choose to use a pipe-cutter, insert the pipe up to the cutting mark and adjust the tension of the cutting wheels

**8** Gradually tighten up the cutting wheels while rotating the pipe-cutter, and continue until the pipe is severed completely

**9** Use the deburring tool accesso to smooth off the inside of the copper tubing and to straighten a crimped edge

elbow with air vent

nged tank connector
th back nut

gate valve

straight coupler
with airvent

equal tee

equal tee

coupling bend

lbow

equal tee

reducing tee

straight coupler

fork tee

reducing tee

corner cross

elbow

straight coupler
with backnut

al tee

slow bend

equal tee

al tee

elbow tee

corner tee

'' tee

stop end

wallplate tee with drain cock

cross

extended coupler

elbow

drain cock

sweep tee

reducing tee

elbow

wallplate elbow

elbow tee

straight coupler
combined with drain plug

thumb tap

elbow

elbow with drain plug

**B.** *A typical selection of compression fittings. These can be classified in four main groups: couplings, tees, crosses, and elbows. Also available are taps, vents, draincocks and stopcocks—sometimes in conjunction with standard fittings. The purpose of couplings and the majority of other fittings is to get round the problems of joining and re-routing copper piping. Slight shape changes in these fittings can have a marked effect on the liquid flow of a system. A fork tee, for instance, is best used when equal-pressure flow division or union is to be made—a function different from a standard tee fitting used to supply a secondary branch of the plumbing system (such as supply of water to a washing machine).*

*Water always takes the easiest course in a system: the low-pressure but wider-bore pipework. Careful use of fittings with a reduced diameter connection—such as the reducing tee—enables the flow of a system to remain mostly undisturbed when the supply is milked. At the same time, the reduced diameter pipework to the appliance from this fitting enables comparatively straightforward—and inexpensive—plumbing.*

*Air vents and drain cocks are fittings you will come across in home central heating systems. Stopcocks can be introduced at the start of every main branch of the plumbing system, so only that branch needs to be disconnected when work is needed on it*

Hayward Art Group

if you cannot get a good finish, leave it and cut the pipe again.

Next remove any swarf (metal shavings) from the outside rim and clean up the inside surface with a round file.

As the edge becomes smooth, angle your file so that you bevel the pipe end slightly (fig.5). Finally, thoroughly clean the finished pipe end with steel wool or a wire brush.

To avoid wastage—and the possibility of mis-measuring—cut and finish one length of pipe before you measure and cut the next.

### Joining the pipe
Copper pipe can either be joined with screw fittings or with soldered joints. Soldered joints are cheaper and have a neater appearance, but they can only be used once the techniques of using a blowlamp have been mastered.

Screw fittings are much easier to use and you are unlikely to need many for a simple pipe run.

The two types of screw, or *compression* fittings used in plumbing are known as *manipulative* and *non-manipulative* (fig. A). The former, which require special tools to flare the pipe ends are rarely used in DIY work. Non-manipulative compression joints are more complicated, but form a good seal once they are assembled. And because they can be taken apart with ease, they also allow you much more flexibility.

### Making a compression joint
To make a compression joint, you need a pair of grips, adjustable wrenches or open-ended spanners, and either a tin of jointing compound or a roll of PTFE tape. The latter is a plastics compound—the PTFE stands for PolyTetraFluoroEthylene—which you wrap around the joint threads to make them watertight.

Make sure the pipe ends to be joined with the fitting are both clean and slightly bevelled. Dismantle the fitting to remove the capnuts and sleeves and place these in order on the piping—setting the sleeves about 12mm from the pipe-ends. If your sleeves are tapered, position them with the slope towards the fitting. If you are using jointing compound, apply this to the inside of each capnut before slipping it on to the pipe-end (fig. 10).

Each pipe in turn is pushed home against the internal stop of the fittings while the capnut is tightened by hand (fig.12). Apply PTFE tape or jointing compound to the male thread on the

fitting before you do this. While you are tightening, be sure not to disturb the seating of the sleeves.

As each capnut is tightened, the sleeve—or compression ring as it is sometimes called—bites into the pipe beneath and spreads out against the nut to form a watertight seal. The degree of tightening is important. Although it is not possible to be precise—follow the manufacturer's suggestion if in doubt—a turn or so after hand-tight is normally sufficient. Over-tightening can cause severe problems.

Where imperial size piping is being attached to a metric fitting or length of piping, the use of additional sealant and tightening is normally quite sufficient to make up for the small differences. In the case of non-manipulative joints careful matching of

sleeve and pipe sizes is necessar you can buy size adaptors—and advice of your local supplier or fessional is worth seeking.

### Compression fittings
A large variety of compression fitti is available (fig. B), enabling all ki of pipe installation to be tackled. for simple projects, you should st to the basic ones—elbows, tees, s bends. If possible, incorporate th into a plan before you visit y builders' or plumbers' merchant. should then be able to advise you whether or not your plan is practi and on possible improvements.

When connecting such a fitti think of it as two, ordinary, comp sion joints and assemble each 'si as described.

**10** *Sealing compound is applied to internal and external surfaces of a non-manipulative joint, ensuring a watertight but adjustable bond*

**11** *The capnut and gland slee are slipped on in logical or and the pipe inserted as far as possible within the fitting*

**12** *While ensuring the pipe remains firmly butted to the internal stop on the fitting, hand-tighten the capnut*

**13** *After hand-tightening, restri use of a spanner to one or t turns to avoid causing damage (fo any specified instruction on this)*

# Simple project: Fitting mixer taps

Replacing troublesome pillar taps with a modern shower/mixer tap set can quickly and cheaply transform the facilities of your bathroom.

In addition to fairly straightforward plumbing the project involves removal and replacement of any bath panelling, fixing of the shower head, and provision of some sort of shower curtain arrangement.

Make sure the water is turned off before you start work, and see that heating is switched off. Trace along pipework to find the stopcocks for both the hot and the cold taps. That for the hot is usually located near to the water heater.

The connection of the new tap set makes use of existing components in the case of older style piping. Remove old taps carefully, noting the arrangement of the components. These are illustrated alongside. The backnut slips loosely along the tail pipe. When this is screwed onto one or other of the shanks of the new tap set, it draws the lipped tail pipe into place. A seal—of hemp or rubber—is sandwiched between the tap shank and pipe-end to make the joint watertight. This seal, usually seated within the end of the tail pipe, must be a replacement. The seating needs a good clean out if jointing compound was used with hemp in the original joint. Repeat the use of jointing compound if hemp is again used.

A straightforward non-manipulative compression joint is all that is needed if you are joining the new tap set directly to copper piping (see below)

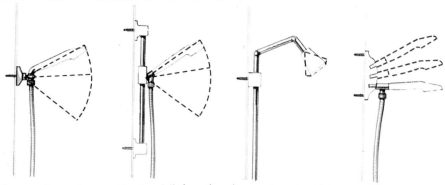

*Some alternative methods of fixing the shower head which may influence your choice of shower/mixer set. A handset is useful for close-quarter rinsing and attaches to the wall usually by a fixed socket (left), slider socket (centre left) or fixed-angle socket (right). Some users prefer a fixed rose (centre right)*

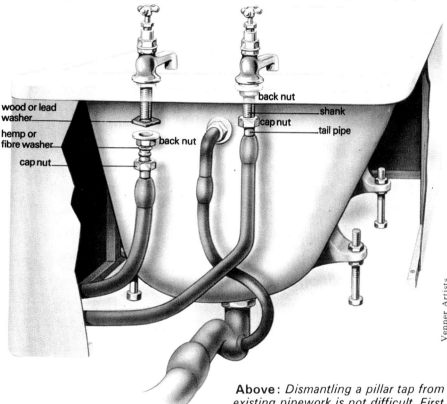

wood or lead washer

hemp or fibre washer

cap nut

back nut

back nut

shank

cap nut

tail pipe

Venner Artists

**Above:** *Dismantling a pillar tap from existing pipework is not difficult. First turn off all water and switch off the heating system. Use a wrench to loosen first the capnut—to disconnect pipe and tap—then the backnut, plus washer, so the tap can be removed from the bath. Reverse the procedure when you fit the mixer set. Use a new hemp or rubber seal before you join the pipe to the shank of the fitting by tightening the capnut*

**Left:** *A modern shower/mixer tap set fits the space of two taps, so check the separation between these before buying. The set comes as a kit complete with shower handset, fitting for this, hose, rubber seating and fittings. Treat pipe fitting to this in exactly the same way as joining pipe to a compression fitting when you are dealing with existing copper pipework*

# Project

# Shelves with a difference

**Alcove shelving should be decorative as well as practical. You can adapt this basic design to any room and any type of decor simply by choosing suitable materials**

Nigel MacIntyre

This alcove shelving system has b specially designed to be as flexible possible and meet all your sl storage requirements.

Based on a simple backing pa made from a series of wooden sl which provide support for the shel the system is easy and cheap to ma You can make the panels as big o small as you like to fit your alcov chimney breast. The system wo just as well on a long wall—sim use as many panels as you need cover the available space and arra the shelves to suit your orname and books.

Each shelf is fixed in place b simple supporting block (see diagrams overleaf) which can ea be unscrewed should you need change the arrangements—as y book collection grows for instance if you want to accommodate a plant or ornament.

The slats allow the shelves to fixed in virtually any position, the visual impact of the slatted v is lost if the shelves are sited too c together.

The illustrations on the oppo page show just a few of the many varied ways you can use the shelv system.

The box shelf at the bottom particularly versatile and can be u as a seat, for instance, by coverin with upholstered foam.

Hinges at the rear of the box al the space underneath to be used general storage or even for hous the hi-fi/record/cassette collect neatly out of the way.

Taking the carpet up the side of box links the wall unit to the res the room visually and adds an atn phere of cosiness and warmth.

The slats can be painted for bright, modern look or varnished a natural finish as shown in picture. You may care to use differ woods on alternate slats for a su decorative effect or choose to pa only a few of the slats and leave rest showing the wood grain.

Any type of wood is suitable either the shelves or the slats, obviously the better the wood better the final appearance, especia if you choose to stain or clear-varn the slats.

Simply follow the working drawi over the page and you can build complete units in less than a day.

# Alternative alcoves

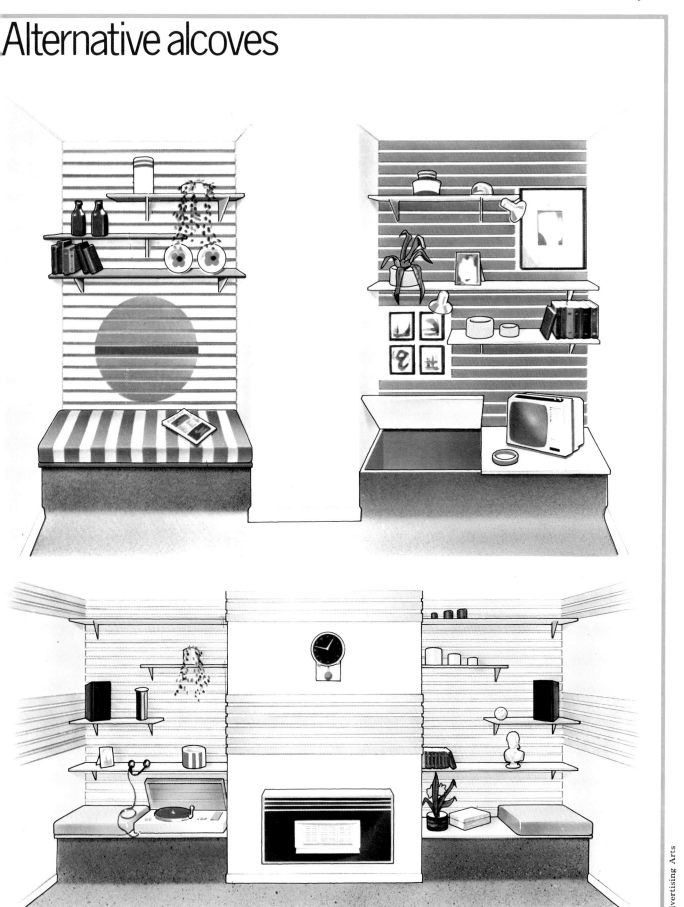

# Workplan

It is important to ensure that the wall you are fixing the shelves to can take the weight of the system.

If you have a brick and plaster wall use wall plugs to secure the support frame to the bricks and use long enough screws and plugs to completely penetrate the plaster layer and bite into the brickwork.

If your wall is the stud and plaster board variety make sure you fasten the holding battens to the studs and not just to the plaster board.

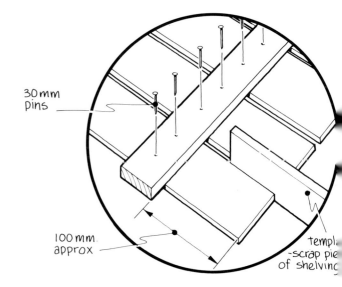

30mm pins

100 mm approx

templ. -scrap pie of shelving

**(1)**

lay the slats on a flat surface and space out.
use a scrap piece of shelving as a template to correctly space the slats.
cut 3 lengths of 25x50mm timber to the required height for uprights.
position two of the uprights approx 100mm from the edges and one in the centre.
pin uprights to slats.

- pin size 30mm

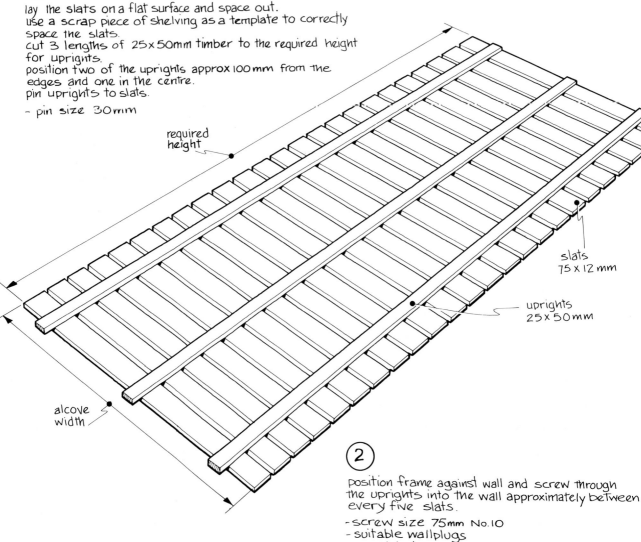

required height

alcove width

slats 75 x 12 mm

uprights 25 x 50mm

**(2)**

position frame against wall and screw through the uprights into the wall approximately between every five slats.

- screw size 75mm No.10
- suitable wallplugs
- use plated screws and cup washers to give a neat appearance

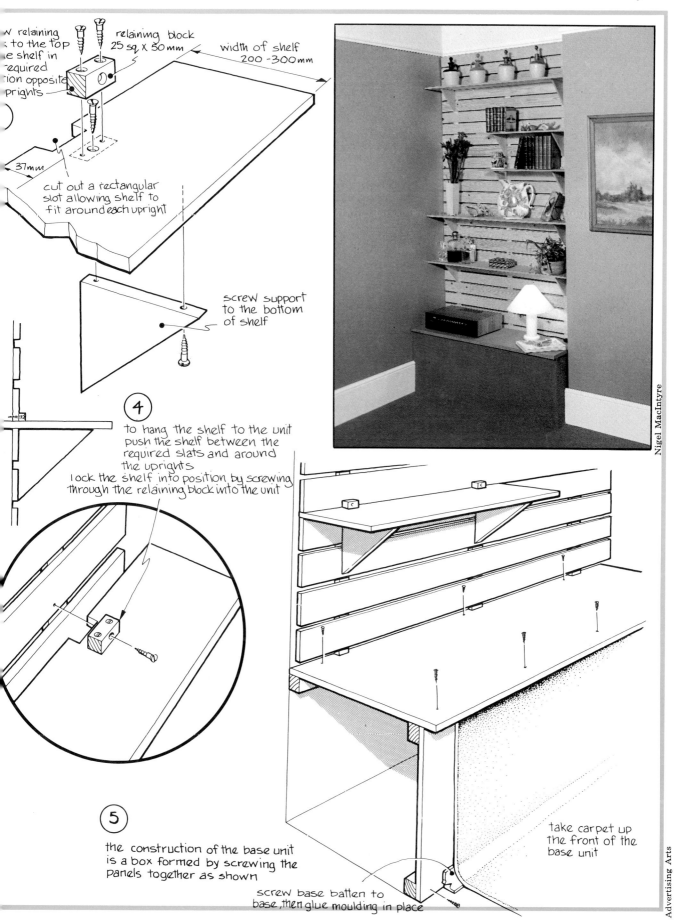

w retaining
s to the top
e shelf in
required
tion opposite
prights

retaining block
25 sq x 50 mm

width of shelf
200-300mm

37mm

cut out a rectangular
slot allowing shelf to
fit around each upright

screw support
to the bottom
of shelf

④

to hang the shelf to the unit
push the shelf between the
required slats and around
the uprights
lock the shelf into position by screwing
through the retaining block into the unit

⑤

the construction of the base unit
is a box formed by screwing the
panels together as shown

screw base batten to
base, then glue moulding in place

take carpet up
the front of the
base unit

Nigel MacIntyre

Advertising Arts

59

# Gutter repairs

**Gutters and downpipes play a vital role in protecting your house from the effects of rain. But unless guttering is regularly maintained it will deteriorate, causing leaks or overflows. The damp in turn causes structural damage which often costs a fortune to repair**

Guttering should be inspected onc twice a year, preferably in late aut and again in the spring. It will alr certainly be necessary to sweep any accumulation of leaves and with a hand brush and trowel or the case of plastic guttering, wit shaped piece of hardboard.

Keep the debris well away from downpipe outlet. If the outlet does have a cage or grille fixed to pre debris from entering and blocking downpipe, roll a piece of wire in ball and insert it in the neck of pipe. Do make sure that the wire is sufficiently large not to fall d the pipe.

With cast-iron guttering, ch carefully for any rust. Use a brush to remove loose flakes of p and rust and treat the surface wi rust inhibitor. The surface sh then be given one or two coats of minous paint to form a strong pro tive layer.

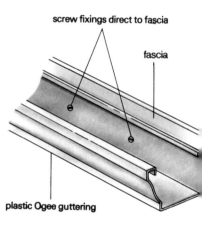

screw fixings direct to fascia

fascia

plastic Ogee guttering

**A.** *Guttering of Ogee-section is screwed directly to the fascia boar*

On Ogee-section guttering (fig. rust may well be found around fixings to the fascia—in which the damaged section must be rem for treatment.

### Clearing blocked downpipes

Before unblocking a downpipe, p plastic bowl or large tin under the of the pipe at the discharge into

**Left:** *Clearing a downpipe. A blockage in a downpipe can caus the system to overflow with damaging results*

Nelson Hargreaves

in to prevent any debris entering drainage system.

When cleaning cast-iron hopper ds, use rubber gloves to protect r hands against sharp edges.

o clear a blockage in a straight ⁄npipe, tie a rag firmly to one end of ⁄ng pole and poke it down the pipe. ⁄e the blockage has been dislodged, h the pipe thoroughly with a hose. ⁄ the downpipe is fitted with a hop-head (fig. B) carefully clear by ⁄d any debris which has collected.

not to compress the debris, or it ⁄ cause further blockage in the ⁄npipe.

With plastic hopper heads, wipe the ⁄de with a cloth and soapy water ⁄e the debris has been cleared.

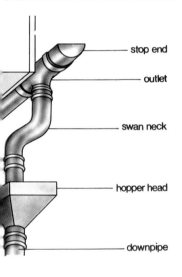

*This downpipe connects to the ⁄ter run via a swan neck*

- stop end
- outlet
- swan neck
- hopper head
- downpipe

With some systems, the guttering is ⁄itioned some way out from the wall ⁄ water is directed into the down-⁄e through an angled section known ⁄ a *swan neck* (fig. B). To clear a ⁄ckage here, use a length of fairly ⁄f wire in place of the pole so that ⁄ bends may be negotiated.

⁄f a blockage is beyond reach, part ⁄all of the downpipe will have to be ⁄mantled.

## ⁄gging gutters

⁄ gutter sags, water may overflow ⁄ the joints may crack and leak. A ⁄ket of water poured in at the high-⁄ point of the system reveals any ⁄h defects.

⁄he commonest causes of sagging ⁄ broken or bent brackets, or loose ⁄ng screws. Most guttering is sup-⁄ted on brackets screwed either to ⁄ fascia boards underneath the

eaves of the roof (fig. C) or to the ends of the roof rafters.

To rectify a sagging gutter, remove the defective sections and examine the brackets to see if they are firmly fixed. If they are not, use longer screws to secure them. Where brackets are bent or corroded, replace them with matching new ones.

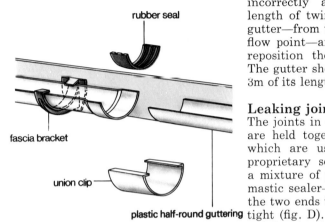

- rubber seal
- fascia bracket
- union clip
- plastic half-round guttering

*C. A section held by a fascia bracket. This joint type is sealed in the socket*

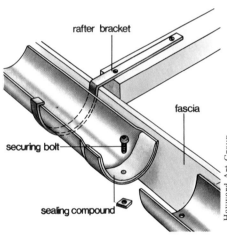

- rafter bracket
- fascia
- securing bolt
- sealing compound

*D. A joint in cast-iron guttering. This gutter is supported by rafter brackets*

Replacing a rafter bracket (fig. D) normally involves removing the slate or tile directly above it, though this problem can often be overcome by fixing a fascia bracket adjacent to the faulty rafter bracket to give the neces-sary extra support.

Ogee section guttering differs from other types in that it is screwed directly on to the fascia. Sagging here is usually caused by the fixing screws rusting and then pulling away from the fascia. In this case, plug the screw holes and fasten with new, galvanized screws.

A common fault with guttering

occurs where the slope or fall towards the downpipe outlet becomes distorted —because of faulty installation or settlement of the house itself. Too steep a fall causes water to overflow at the downpipe outlet. Too shallow a one results in a build up of water and sediment along the run.

To determine the correct fall for an incorrectly aligned section, tie a length of twine along the top of the gutter—from the high end to the out-flow point—and use it as a guide to reposition the intervening brackets. The gutter should fall 25mm for every 3m of its length.

## Leaking joints in cast-iron

The joints in cast-iron gutter systems are held together by nuts and bolts which are usually screw-headed. A proprietary sealing compound—often a mixture of putty and red lead or a mastic sealer—is sandwiched between the two ends to make the joint water-tight (fig. D).

A leaking joint may be patched up by cleaning the area with a wire brush and applying one or two coats of bituminous paint. However, for a more permanent repair the section on one side of the leaking joint must be removed, cleaned and replaced. If the removed piece is in the middle of a run, two new joints have to be made —one at each end of the section.

Start by removing the bolts which hold the joints together. These may well have rusted and seized—in which case apply penetrating oil to loosen them. If this fails, saw through the bolts with a junior hacksaw. With Ogee-section guttering, remove the screws holding the section to the fascia as well (fig. 1).

Lift out the loosened section—making sure as you do so that its weight does not catch you off balance —and take it to the ground (fig. 2). Returning to the guttering, chip off all traces of old sealing compound from the hanging end (fig. 3) and scour it thoroughly with a wire brush. Repeat the cleaning operation on the removed section (figs 4 and 5).

Apply fresh sealing compound to the socket section of the joint, spread-ing it in an even layer about 6mm thick (fig. 6). Relocate the removed gutter section, screwing it to the fascia or laying it on its brackets and fitting the joints together.

Insert a new galvanized bolt into the joint from above (fig. 7). Screw on its securing nut, tightening gently so that the joint closes up and squeezes out any excess compound (fig. 8). Trim away the excess with a putty knife

Hayward Art Group

# Repairs and renovations

**1** *This leaking section of cast-iron guttering is on the end of a run. The guttering is secured by screws in the fascia rather than by brackets*

**2** *When the bolt in the joint at the other end of the section has been loosened and removed, you can pull the section away from the wall*

**3** *The leak is at the joint with the adjoining section. Using hamme and screwdriver, gently chip off trac of old sealing compound*

**4** *Repeat the cleaning operation for the section that has been removed. Scrape off old sealing compound from the joint end*

**5** *When the old sealing compound has been removed, scour clean the two ends of the joint thoroughly with a wire brush*

**6** *Apply new sealing compound t the socket section of the joint, spread in an even layer about 6mm thick over the socket area*

**7** *Having replaced the removed section and fitted the joint together, take a new bolt and insert it in the hole in the joint from above*

**8** *Screw the securing nut onto the end of the bolt and tighten with screwdriver and spanner so that joint closes and squeezes out compound*

**9** *Use a putty knife to trim away all excess sealing compound squeezed onto the surface during the tightening process*

(figs 9 and 10), wipe over the area with a damp rag, then repeat the operation for the other joint. Finally, paint the joints with one or two coats of bituminous paint.

## Making joints in plastics

Leaks from plastics guttering can be just as damaging as those from cast-iron and should be attended to as soon as possible.

In most plastics guttering systems, the sections are connected by union clips, lined with replaceable rubber seals (fig. E). In some cases, the seal is positioned in the end of one section of gutter with a separate clip used to secure the joint (fig. C). When the clips are sprung home, the gutter ends compress against the pad to form a watertight joint—but this can leak if silt finds its way in.

To replace a seal, undo the clip holding the ends together, lift out the old seal and thoroughly clean the surfaces which come into contact with it. Fit a new seal of the same type and snap the joint back together by squeezing the ends of the gutter slightly and snapping the union clip over each edge of the section.

In some plastics guttering systems, sections of guttering are cemented together in narrow union clips (fig. F). To repair such a joint, you will need a new, matching section of gutter about 300mm long, some solvent cement and two new union clips.

Use a try square to mark cutting lines about 300mm from either side of the leaking joint, then cut along one of the lines with a hacksaw. Stick masking tape along the cut and cut along the second line so that the section containing the joint is severed.

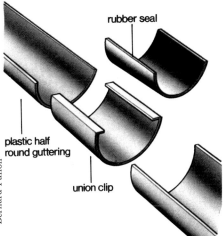

E. *This section of plastics guttering is connected by a sealed union clip*

O *Trim all the excess compound on the lower part of the joint well. Give the new joint a wipe with a damp rag before painting*

Bernard Fallon

Unclip the cut section from the gutter brackets, remove it and use it for sizing up the new piece.

Apply solvent cement to one side of both new union clips and fit a clip to each end. Now slide the outlet end of the existing gutter—which is always left unsealed to allow for expansion and contraction—along to give room to position the new section.

Apply a further layer of cement to the clip which mates with other end of the run and join the new section. Finally, cement the other clip and slide the outlet end of the gutter back to mate with it.

On systems which use combined union brackets, silt bridged joints are used (fig. G). The silt bridge clips into the union to prevent debris working its way into the joint and causing leaks. Leaks in such joints will be due to cracks—either in the bridge or in the union bracket itself—and can be remedied by replacing the defective part with a matching new one.

To fit a new silt bridge, hook one end under the front of the union clip and snap the other end under the lip at the back of the gutter.

## Replacing a cast-iron section

If the whole system has eroded, it may be advisable to replace it with plastics guttering.

However, if the rest of the run is still in good condition, replacing a corroded cast-iron section is well worthwhile.

Where possible, take the old section to a builder's merchant and obtain a matching replacement. As well as the shape and diameter, check that the new section matches the existing joints. If not, buy the appropriate union at the same time.

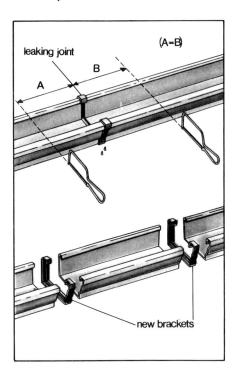

F. *A leak in this type of joint can be repaired only by replacing the section*

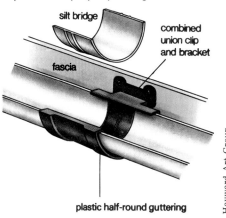

Hayward Art Group

G. *The joint in this gutter is sealed by a silt bridge clipped into the union*

Cast-iron guttering is normally sold in 1.8mm lengths, so the new section may have to be cut to fit. When measuring it up, take into account any overlap for the joints or new joint unions.

To cut it, lay the old section over the top of the new and use it as a guide. Mark the new section in pencil and lay a strip of masking tape along the mark, towards the waste side, to give a clearer guide. Cut the section with a large hacksaw.

Mark the positions of the joint bolt holes and punch and drill them to a diameter of 8mm before you fit the new section into place.

# Repairs and renovations

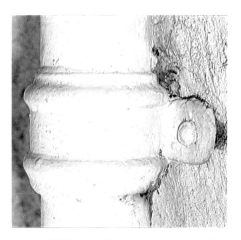

**11** *This cast-iron downpipe section is attached to the wall by pipe nails driven into wooden plugs which have become loose*

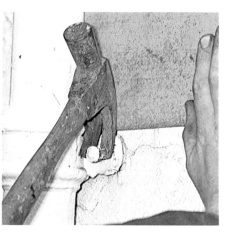

**12** *Remove the nails by levering them out with a claw hammer. To obtain leverage, hold an offcut of timber against the wall*

**13** *With the pipe nails removed, pull away the lower section. Joints sealed with compound will have to be loosened first*

**14** *Having dug the loose plugs out of the masonry, extend the holes with a 12mm masonry drill to make sure replacement plugs fit*

**15** *Using a hammer, firmly drive your replacement wooden plugs into the holes until they are flush. Make sure the plugs are firm*

### Cast-iron downpipe repairs

Cast-iron downpipes are usually a tached to walls by pipe nails driv into metal, lead or wood plugs. T nails run through cast metal bracke (fig. 11) some of which have space behind to prevent contact between t pipe and the wall. Brackets often co loose, making the pipe dangerous.

To secure a loose bracket, start removing the bracket nearest to t ground and repeat the operation up and including the bracket that loose. To remove a bracket, lever c the nails with a claw hammer (fig. 1 Use an offcut of timber held agai the wall to obtain the necessa leverage. Withdraw the section downpipe (fig. 13). Where the join have been sealed and do not fall aw easily, heat them with a blow lamp loosen the sealing compound or ch the compound away by hand.

Remove the loose plugs by diggi them out of the masonry, and make replacements—slightly larger round than the holes—from pieces 12mm dowel. If necessary, extend t holes with a 12mm masonry drill (f 14). Drive the replacement plugs in the wall until they are flush (fig. 1 check that they are firm, then re the downpipe (fig. 16).

In many houses, downpipe joints a unsealed. If dirt collects in an unsea joint, water may gather and free and crack the pipe. Avoid this filling any unsealed joints with mixture of red lead and putty or proprietary mastic. Wipe it smoc with a rag (fig. 17) then seal the jo with a coat of bituminous paint. the same with sealed joints that ha become loose, having first chipped the old compound.

**16** *When both plugs have been fitted, replace the lower section so that the bracket holes are level with the plugs. Hammer in two new nails*

**17** *To prevent the downpipe cracking, force some fresh jointing compound into the joint, then wipe it smooth with a rag*

# Bathroom problems solved

hatever the problem in your bathroom, there
bound to be a way round it. And quite often,
is the simplest solutions which bring about
e most startling transformations

holder and a brown plastic-framed mirror will complete the look and tone down the harsh qualities of the sanitary fittings.

A white bathroom suite is enlivened by covering the walls with a patterned wallpaper which has a white background. Sealed cork flooring can then be laid and run up the sides of the bath to hide the back or side panels, adding warmth to the room.

The blind or curtains could be in a design which matches the wallpaper, or in an accent colour such as bright green. With white sanitaryware, the accessories and towels will predominate: these could all be in one strong colour such as burgundy or green.

If the sanitaryware is in a pale lemon, depth can be added to the colour by tiling the splashbacks with mustard-coloured tiles and choosing a wallpaper which has the same mustard shade in its pattern. Cork tiles or fawn carpeting could be used to cover the floor and sides of the bath. Brown curtains or blinds combined with pine accessories such as towel rail, shelf and bath rack will

**Left**: *An old-fashioned bathroom suite which has been boxed-in and decorated in such a way that the eye is immediately distracted upwards*

**Below**: *An unusual tap arrangement, plus ingenious use of sealed cork tiles as a wall covering and splashback bring a traditional white suite to life*

## isguising old fittings

oving into a new home often means
at you have also inherited a modern
throom suite in a pale colour which
u do not like. But clever use of
coration and accessories can either
derplay the colour of the suite by
awing attention away from it, or
e make it seem a warmer shade.

If your bathroom has pale pink
nitaryware, give it a more sophisti-
ted look by choosing a patterned
llpaper containing dusky pink as
predominant colour. Cover the floor
th a washable brown carpet, run-
ng it up the sides of the bath.

If the wallpaper has a co-ordinating
bric, make blinds or curtains in this
or from a dusky pink or deep brown
bric. Brown accessories, such as
th rack, soap dish, toothbrush

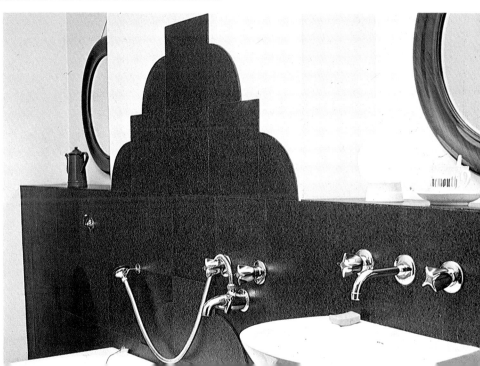

make the suite seem bolder.

A sky blue bathroom suite can be made to seem deeper and more dramatic by covering the walls in either deep blue tiles or a deep blue patterned wallpaper. Flooring could be in a shade such as beige—carried up the sides of the bath—and matched to deep blue plastic accessories, beige towels and deep blue bath set.

## Accessories

Although renewing the decorations is the most obvious way of changing the face of a bathroom, equipping it with new accessories can be just as effective and certainly requires less effort. The accessories can be used to colour co-ordinate with the sanitaryware giving your bathroom a certain 'look' —bold and vibrant; streamlined and efficient; contemporary; or even a look which is predominantly female. It may have to be a family decision.

Bill McLaughlin

**Below**: *Colour-matched accessories give a small bathroom an uncluttered appearance, especially if the towels are chosen to harmonize*

**Above**: *A standard toilet made far from ordinary. The walls and window are plain but the paper-holder and painting add a touch of class*

A huge range of fitments—in met ceramic and plastic—is available fro department stores, chain stores a specialist bathroom shops. You c buy not only a whole range of acc sories in one colour and style, b colour matched towels and bath ma as well. In a large bathroom there scope for mixing the colour of acc sories but in a small one, matchi accessories are easier on the eye.

If sanitaryware has passed its pri in terms of appearance but still fun tions perfectly, you can impro things by using clever disguise tacti **The bath:** Boxing-in an unattracti bath can drastically improve appearance. Hardboard can be fitt around the bath underneath the and then decorated with paint wallpaper—sealed with polyuretha varnish to protect it from splash Alternatively, floor coverings su as sealed cork, vinyl or carpeting c be continued from the floor right the sides of the bath.

Rather than trying to disguise old bath which has cast-iron legs ball and claw feet, you can make i feature of the bathroom by painti the outside in a bold colour or sten ling on an eye-catching design. T addition of new taps can give the ba an updated, or cared-for look.

If the inside of a cast-iron bath in a bad condition it can be paint with an enamel bath paint—althou this is not always very successf It is better just to clean the bath w an extra-strong cleaning agent.

Where the bathroom has old sa taryware it is sensible to choo 'classic' style decoration which w blend sympathetically with the sui Carefully chosen, a marbled or e bossed paper will add an unmistaka 'vintage' character to a bathroom useful if you are trying to make t most of old wall tiles.

**The basin:** An unsightly wash bas can be largely hidden by building vanity unit around it. This will n only smarten up the basin—hidi the plumbing underneath—but a provide storage space for toilet req sites. Again, new taps can be add for an improved appearance, as car new plug and chain.

**The wc:** An old high-level ciste can be disguised by building a cu board around it, with a hole drill in the base for the chain and hand A new chain and handle will h and the wc seat can easily be replac by bolting on a new one. The additi of a new seat cover and pedestal m always give the wc a fresh lease life.

Crayonne

## ack of space

ere space in a bathroom is limited,
 illusion of extra space can be
ated by careful choice of decor.
ere are three principal ways to
ually enlarge a room—by using
our, by carefully arranging the
ll decoration or by using mirrors.

'ale colours cause the walls to
cede', making the overall space
ear correspondingly larger, while
ght dominant shades tend to bring
 walls closer together.

he same is true when choosing
terned wallpaper or tiles for the
lls of a small bathroom—a small
tern in a muted colour makes the
m seem larger while a bold pattern
a bright colour overwhelms small
ms and creates an oppressive,
ustrophobic effect.

Hanging wallpaper horizontally is
 another way of creating an illu-

**low**: *Even dark colours can make*
*mall bathroom seem spacious.*
*amatic use of bright fittings and*
*e clean lines of the tiles add a*
*se of space*

sion of extra space, linear-patterned
wallpapers being the most effective.
This technique can also be employed
to seemingly alter the shape of the
room, using horizontal wallpaper on
just one or two walls.

Mirrors give a more solid illusion
of enlarged space. As an added bonus,
they make a dark room seem lighter
by reflecting whatever space is available around the room. On an end
wall, a large mirror makes the bathroom seem twice as long: a large
mirror on a side wall makes the room
look twice as wide. In a steamy bathroom use an acrylic mirror which has
been specially coated to resist misting.

Mirror tiles, either tinted or plain,
are another sensible choice for the
bathroom. Easy to fix to the wall—
they have adhesive pads at the back
of them—they are easier to handle
than a large sheet mirror. And because
the joints break up reflected images,
they can be used more extensively
without fear of having your reflection
follow you around. Like all mirrors,
mirror tiles should be fitted so that
air can flow behind them—damp tends
to ruin mirror finishes.

## Ugly pipework

Old bathrooms often contain a great
deal of ugly pipework in need of disguising. This can either be done by
boxing in the exposed pipes, or by
fitting wood panelling over them.

As wood panelling can be secured
to almost anything—including old
ceramic tiles and chipped walls—it is
an effective way of disguising pipework as well as being an attractive form
of decoration. The panelling can be
applied vertically, horizontally or
diagonally for an interesting effect
with the timber stained in various
shades of the same colour.

An alternative way to approach
the problem of exposed pipes is to
actually make them a feature of the
room by picking the pipework out in
bright, strong colours.

Susan Griggs

**Above**: *When ugly pipework is*
*given a vivid treatment, it is*
*transformed into the main feature*

The Picture Library

**Above**: *A quick way to liven up a*
*bath and hide its plumbing—matching*
*shutters complete the look*

## Storage problems

In a small bathroom every bit of spare space may need to be untilized for storing things.

**Open shelves:** Open shelving—made from materials such as sealed or painted solid timber or melamine-faced chipboard—can be used satisfactorily to store many items. Glass needs to be kept spotlessly clean to look its best.

Narrow shelves can be fitted in many places in a bathroom, such as along the wall side of the bath; above the bath taps; above the wc cistern; and even between the wc bowl and cistern. Take care when storing breakable items such as glass bottles and jars on shelves above the wash basin as they could chip or shatter the enamel if they fell.

**Bath:** Where the bath rim is wide enough, it makes a convenient place to store toiletries and manicure implements. Another way of utilizing bath space as storage is to box round the bath as shown on pages 70-71.

**Basin:** Building a vanitory unit

**Above**: *If you have nowhere to put things, flaunt them as brazenly as the bathroom permits*

around a basin provides a logical place to store toiletries with the added advantage that plumbing and waste pipes are hidden. Drawbacks are that water tends to lie on the surface of the unit in puddles while the edge detail between basin and surface often becomes grimy.

**Medicine cabinets:** Mirror-fronted cabinets are sold in a variety of materials, including pine, enamelled steel and coloured plastic and many are included in co-ordinated accessory ranges. Some cabinets have fluorescent lighting above the mirror, shaving sockets, drawers and shelves, and items such as toothbrush racks fitted inside them. They can be used to store toiletries as well as medicines.

If there are children in the household, the cabinet will either have to be lockable or else designed to make it impossible for a child to open. Do not position a medicine cabinet anywhere prone to condensation.

## Cold and damp

A bathroom which has a cold floor both to the touch and appearance not only makes the room look clinic but also shocks the senses when ea morning bare feet come into cont with it. A floorcovering which is s to the touch and easy on the eye w make the bathroom a more comfo able place and create a feeling cosiness and warmth.

The idea of carpeting a bathroom often dismissed as being impractic both because of the expense a because of the amount of water like to be splashed around. Howeve synthetic fibre carpeting—in materi such as acrylic and nylon—is sold a number of manufacturers. This h a synthetic or rubber backing whi does not absorb water—and cons quently does not rot. For a luxurio look, the carpeting can be extend up the sides of the bath.

Vinyl floorings—sold in both she and tile form—are relatively soft und foot and come in a wide variety patterns and colours. They, too, c extended up the sides of the bath to e the back and side panels. The atest advantage of vinyl flooring

low: *Coldness has been nished from this bathroom by ng warm colours*

is that it is easily cleaned and does not require polishing.

Sealed cork tiles add a warm touch to a cold-looking bathroom and like other tiles, can be taken up onto the walls and surfaces around baths and wash hand-basins.

Where a bathroom has a solid flooring such as ceramic tiles, it can be 'softened' by the addition of a cotton, tumble-twist rug. These are available in a variety of shades to colour co-ordinate with your bathroom decor and can be taken up and machine washed.

Condensation is often the biggest single problem in a bathroom, especially where gloss paint and ceramic tiles have been used on the walls. An extractor fan copes effectively with this by carrying the water-laden air away before it condenses. It has the added advantage of keeping the room fresh, dispensing with the need to keep the window open. But because it carries out a lot of warm air, an extractor fan is not suited to a bathroom which is already cold.

Condensation can also be minimized by keeping the bathroom warm and if you have not got central heating, a wall fire or heated towel rail combined with warm furnishings should help. Wall fires must be operated by a pull switch and should be fitted high enough to comply with the regulations in your locality.

The limitations set by your heating and ventilation should be considered when you are choosing decorations. An attractive stone floor will be unbearably cold without underfloor heating. Likewise, metallic-papered walls will create endless condensation problems without proper ventilation.

## oblems with tiles

ere bathroom walls have been ed, they may be chipped and cked. Or, if they have been used y for splash surfaces and window ges, they may leave random shapes.

f you decide to replace the tiles you st remove the old ones and make d the wall underneath. However, noving old tiles often involves re work than is anticipated and u may prefer just to replace individal damaged tiles.

An economical way of disguising es which are basically sound but ok dingy is to paint them with two three coats of vinyl gloss in a ade to match the decor.

Alternatively, you could stencil patns on individual tiles at regular tervals. Stick-on plastic tile covers, a variety of patterns, easily and ectively hide less-than-perfect tiles.

ght: *Lift dull, white tiles from eir clinical level with bold use of ster colours and a dramatic rangement of coloured tiles*

Elizabeth Whiting

# Space-saving storage

Gavin Cochrane

**Above and left:** *The comp project in soft, neutral colours blend beautifully with the bath which allow any number of colo accessories to be displayed. Note neatly the sliding door arrange has been extended underneath tiles. The space created here ca used for dirty washing or other room effects such as spare paper or washing powder.*

use high rebate so doors can be r
by lifting and pulling outward

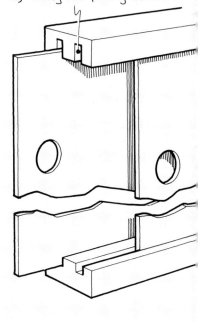

One of the most irritating features of a small bathroom is the lack of storage space. In this design, every bit of space is put to good use. The area surrounding the bath has been boxed off with sliding doors and can be used for storing such unsightly items as floor cloths and other cleaning materials.

An inset section in the wall has been created by constructing a simple framework of softwood battens, then screwing chipboard sheets over the top. This makes an ideal surface on which to lay ceramic tiles.

The glass shelves set into the tiled alcove can display some of the more attractive bathroom accessories: bottles of perfume, boxes of soap, storage jars full of crystals or plants. Alternatively, they make ideal storage space for all the clutter which tends to accumulate round the edges of the bath and wash hand-basin.

A great advantage of the design is that it can be easily adapted to suit your own personal needs—all you need to do is choose tiles and paint which match the existing decor.

On the other hand, you could use the design as the basis for giving your bathroom a completely new look—perhaps with a raised-up bath.

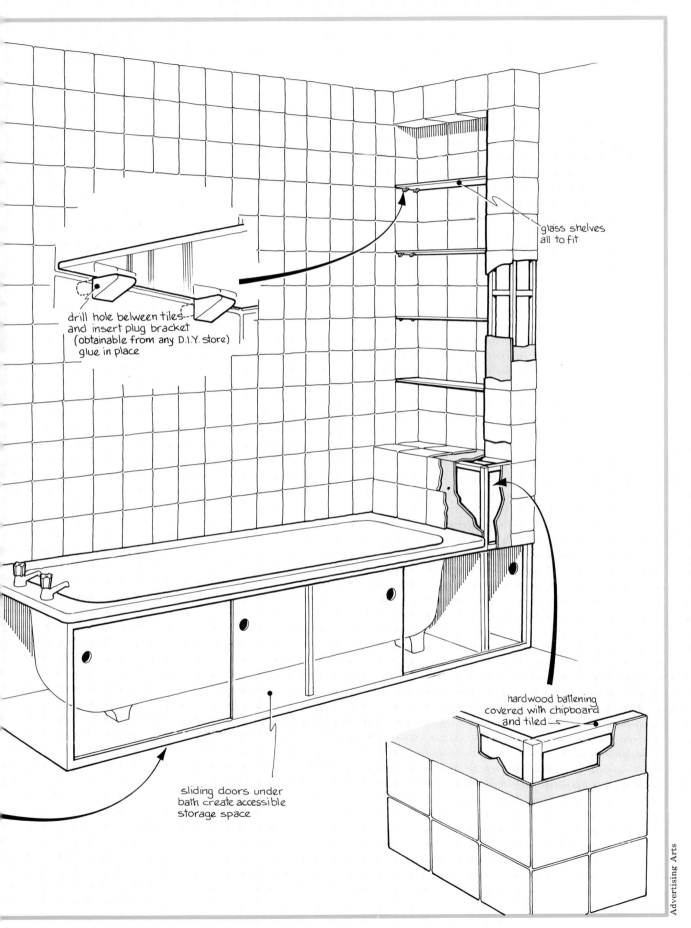

glass shelves all to fit

drill hole between tiles and insert plug bracket (obtainable from any D.I.Y. store) glue in place

hardwood battening covered with chipboard and tiled

sliding doors under bath create accessible storage space

# Fixing wood to wood

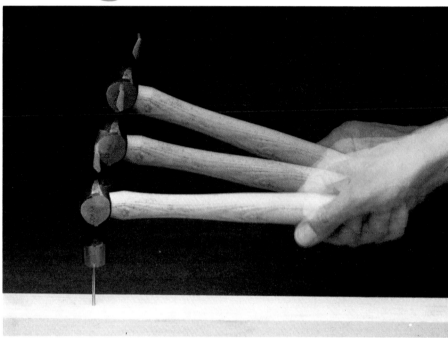

For burying nails below the surf: of the wood, you need a set of r punches. These come in various si —to suit different sizes of nail—a help to avoid bruising the wood w the hammer head.

Some kind of drill is essential screwing work. A power drill is obvious choice because of its ver tility but where there are no po points or access is limited, a wh brace (fig 9) may prove invaluable.

Together with a set of woodwork:

**The correct tools ● Using a hammer ● Nailing tips ● Removing nails ● Drilling screw holes ● Drilling techniques ● Countersinking ● Driving screws ● Nail and screw buying guides**

Nails and screws are the two most important fastening devices used in carpentry, but how well they do their job depends almost entirely on how correctly they are used.

### Tools

For simple nailing work, only a hammer is essential. The two used most frequently in carpentry are the claw hammer and the cross-pein, or 'Warrington'. The first is useful for levering out old nails and lifting floorboards while the second is more suited to finer nailing work.

If you are starting a tool kit, opt for a 450g claw hammer and a 280g Warrington. Later, you can add a 100g 'pin' Warrington for light, accurate nailing and pinning.

**1** *If you are drilling large holes by hand, use a swing brace. When the point emerges, turn the wood over and drill from the other side*

**2** *Start short nails with a cross-pein hammer. Tap gently with the wedge end until they stand firm then drive in with the hammer face*

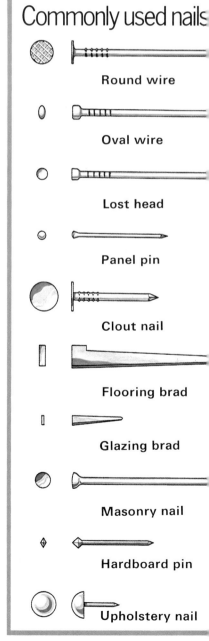

## Commonly used nails

Round wire

Oval wire

Lost head

Panel pin

Clout nail

Flooring brad

Glazing brad

Masonry nail

Hardboard pin

Upholstery nail

st drills, these two tools should
e care of most small and medium
d screwing jobs. To drill larger
es by hand, you need a swing brace
 1) and a set of special bits—
 a priority for the beginner's
ic tool kit.

or screw holes into softwood below
. 6 gauge (3.5mm) and for rough
rk, a bradawl can be used instead
the drill and bit.

ood quality screwdrivers are essen-
 to any tool kit and cabinet screw-
vers, with blades of about 300mm,
 the most useful. Two of them—
 with an 8mm tip and one with a
mm tip—should cover you for most

jobs. To deal with crosshead, Philips
or Posidriv screws, you need screwdrivers with the appropriate tips.

Ratchet and pump-action screwdrivers are also available. But
although they often save time and
effort, they are by no means essential.

## Using a hammer

Using a hammer properly requires a
little bit of practice. Take a firm grip
at the end of the handle and form
your arm into a right-angle, looking
straight down on the work as you do
so. Start the nail by tapping it lightly,
keeping your wrist controlled but
flexible and letting the hammer head
do the work. Increase the power of
your stroke slightly as the nail goes
in but at no time let your arm waver—
if you do, you will either miss, or
bend, the nail.

On well-finished work, remember
not to drive nails right in—leave a
bit protruding for the hammer and
nail punch to finish off.

Start light nails or tacks with the
cross-pein by tapping gently with the
wedge end of the hammer head. Drive

them home with the hammer face
using a number of fairly gentle taps
rather than trying to knock them in
with one blow, which will probably
bend the nail. Very short nails can
be held with a pair of thin-nosed
pliers until they stand on their own.

Hammer faces should be kept clean,
smooth and free from grease: a
slippery or damaged hammer causes
accidents. If possible, polish your
hammer heads on a piece of medium
emery cloth before use.

## Nailing techniques

For accurate, well-finished work, nails
alone do not normally make a strong
joint. However, if the nails are angled
in opposition to each other, a reason-
able joint can be made. When used in
conjunction with one of the modern,
woodworking adhesives, a very strong
joint can be achieved. The panel on
page 74 shows some common nailing
techniques. Seldom are nails driven
straight—a stronger joint can be made
if they go in at an angle or *skew*.

When nailing two pieces of wood
together, nail the smaller to the

---

rough carpentry work: large
y head ensures a firm grip.
ble to split wood

mmonly used in carpentry.
al cross section makes it
ikely to split wood if the long
s follows the grain

neral carpentry nail. Head can
punched below surface and
hole filled

all nail for securing light
ces of wood; usually used in
junction with glue

ge headed for fixing roofing
, sash cords, wire fencing to
od. Galvanized for outdoor
rk

ed to hold down floorboards.
od holding power and unlikely
split wood

adless: used to hold glass to
ture frames and lino to
orboards. Will not grip if
ven too far in

rdened steel nail for fixing
od to soft brick, breeze block
d concrete

ecial head shape countersinks
lf in hardboard and can be
ed over

corative head used to cover
ks in upholstery work

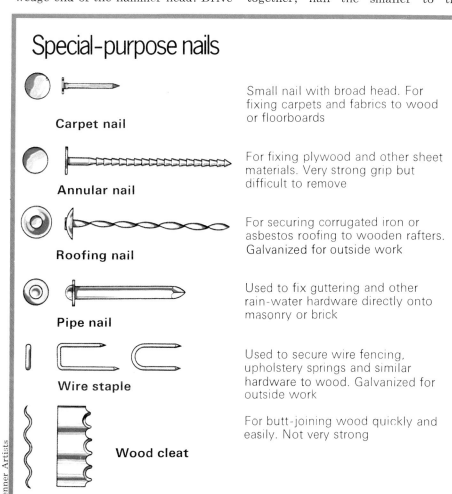

## Special-purpose nails

**Carpet nail**
Small nail with broad head. For
fixing carpets and fabrics to wood
or floorboards

**Annular nail**
For fixing plywood and other sheet
materials. Very strong grip but
difficult to remove

**Roofing nail**
For securing corrugated iron or
asbestos roofing to wooden rafters.
Galvanized for outside work

**Pipe nail**
Used to fix guttering and other
rain-water hardware directly onto
masonry or brick

**Wire staple**
Used to secure wire fencing,
upholstery springs and similar
hardware to wood. Galvanized for
outside work

**Wood cleat**
For butt-joining wood quickly and
easily. Not very strong

Venner Artists

Venner Artists

## Nailing tips

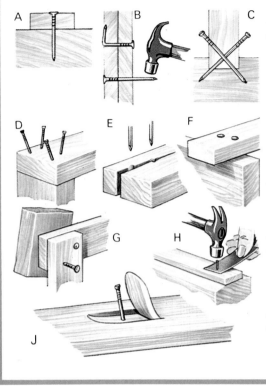

**A**. Use nails about 3 times as long as the workpiece. Always nail smaller to larger. **B**. On rough work, clench-nailed joints are much stronger. **C**. Skew-nailing is one of the best ways of securing a housing joint. **D**. When nailing into end-grain, drive in nails at opposing angles. **E**. Driving more than one nail along the same grain line risks splitting the wood. **F**. Nail small battens overlength to avoid splitting the end. Afterwards, saw or plane off the excess. **G**. Avoid 'bouncing' by placing a block under the workpiece. **H**. Small nails can be positioned with the aid of a cardboard holder. **J**. Secret nailing. Prise up a sliver of timber with a chisel. Glue down after nailing

**3** Very small nails and pins should be held with a pair of pliers. Use the cross-pein hammer hit the nail with fairly gentle taps

**4** Use the claw hammer to remov any partially driven nails. Slide the claw under the nail head then give it several short, sharp pulls

larger. Avoid nailing into hardwoods altogether: if you must, drill a pilot hole first, slightly smaller than the shank of the nail.

### Removing nails

The claw hammer is used to remove partially driven nails. To avoid damaging the surface of the wood, place a small offcut under the hammer head before you start levering (fig 5). Extract nails with a number of pulls rather than trying to do the job in one.

Use pincers to remove small nails and pins which are difficult to grip with the claw hammer—a nail without a head, for example.

If a nail is impossible to remove, punch it below the surface of the wood and use filler to cover the hole, or carefully chip away some of the wood around the head until you can get a grip on the nail head with a pair of pincers.

### Drilling screw holes

All screws must have pilot holes made before they can be driven home. For screws into softwood smaller than No. 6 gauge (3.5mm), make these with a bradawl. Drive into the wood with its chisel point across the grain, to avoid splitting.

Screws into hardwood and screws into softwood larger than No. 6 gauge need two pilot holes. One for the thread—the pilot hole—and one for the shank—the shank hole. These must be made with a drill and bit.

For all except the largest pilot holes, use twist drill bits. Those for pilot holes should be the same size as the screw core to which the threads are attached. Those for the shanks should match the screw shanks exactly. If you buy a set of twist drills, these will cover you for all screw sizes in common use.

When drilling pilot holes, mark the required depth on the drill bit with a piece of masking tape. This will tell you when to stop and cannot damage the workpiece should you overdrill.

As with nailing, where two pieces of wood are to be fixed together, screw the smaller to the larger. Drill the shank hole right through the smaller piece so it is pulled down tight as the screw is driven home. If the shank hole goes only part of the way through you will find it very hard to pull the top piece of wood down tight and may risk breaking or damaging the screw. Brute force should never be used—it indicates that either the thread hole or the shank hole is too small.

### Countersinking

Countersinking is normally the easi way of recessing screw heads fl with, or below the surface of the wo The recess is made with a countersi bit (fig 7) after the pilot has be drilled, to the same depth as countersunk screw head. Take p ticular care if you are countersink with a power drill or the recess m accidentally become too large.

For some screw sizes, special l are available to drill the thread ho shank hole and countersink recess one operation. Care should be tak however, as they break easily.

### Drilling techniques

Using the correct drilling techni makes all the difference to the qua of the finished work. Whether y drill is power or hand operated, y should always hold it at right ang to the work surface so that the pi hole is straight. If you find this d cult, rest a try square upright next the bit and use it as a guide.

**5** To remove large nails and to avoid damaging the wood, slip block of wood under the head of nail. This increases the leverage

**6** Use pincers to remove nails which are difficult to grip with a claw hammer. A series of sharp pulls avoids leaving a large hole

**7** For flat-head countersunk screws, use a countersink bit. Drill a hole of the same diameter as that of the screw head

## Screws: types and uses

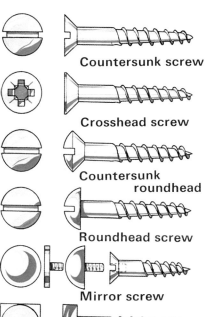

**Countersunk screw**

Used for general woodwork. The head sinks in flush with or slightly below the wood surface

**Crosshead screw**

Used for general woodwork, but needs a special screwdriver which does not slip from the head

**Countersunk roundhead**

Used for fixing door-handle plates and other decorative fittings with countersunk holes. The head is designed to be seen

**Roundhead screw**

Used for fixing hardware fittings without countersunk holes. The head protrudes from the work

**Mirror screw**

Used for fixing mirrors and bathroom fittings. The chromed cap threads into the screw head to hide the screw. Do not overtighten

**Nuthead screw**

Used for fixing heavy constructions together and heavy equipment to timbers. Tighten with a spanner

**Invisible screw**

Used for invisible joining of two pieces of timber.

**Panel screw**

Used for fixing thin sheets of metal and plastic. Cuts its own thread as it is screwed in. Various types of head are available

**Chipboard screw**

Used for securing chipboard and its derivatives

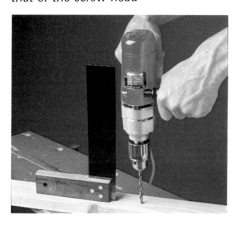

**8** Always hold a drill at right-angles to the surface so that you drill a straight hole. Rest a try square next to the bit and use it as a guide

**A.** Think of screws as being in sections and drill the pilot holes accordingly

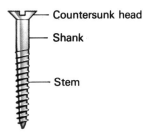

— Countersunk head

— Shank

— Stem

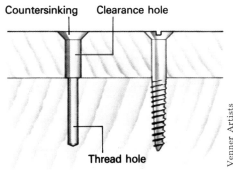

Countersinking    Clearance hole

Thread hole

**9** *When you are drilling horizontally with a hand-operated wheel brace, grip the handle with your thumb towards the wheel*

**10** *A pump action screwdriver should be held with both hands. Make sure the screwdriver is squarely on the screw head*

Always use a power drill with the cable over your shoulder, where it cannot accidentally become damaged or interfere with the work.

With bit drills, operate the drill in bursts and lift it frequently to allow debris to escape. To give yourself as much control as possible, always hold the drill with both hands and never press too hard—you are bound to overdrill.

Keep the chuck key taped to the cable, so it is handy whenever you want to change bits.

Using a hand-operated wheel brace requires slightly more effort, but gives more control than a power drill. When drilling vertically, grip the handle with your thumb on top. Turn the wheel steadily to avoid knocking the drill out of line.

To drill horizontally, grip the handle with your thumb towards the wheel (fig 9). Alternatively, where a side handle is fitted, grasp this in one hand while you turn the wheel steadily with the other.

Avoid applying excessive body pressure to the wheel brace at all times or you will snap the bits.

### Driving screws
Always make sure that the tip of your screwdriver is in good condition and that it fits exactly into the slot in the screw head. A blade which is too narrow or rounded damages the slot, while too wide a blade damages the wood as the screw goes in.

As a time-saving alternative to the conventional screwdriver, a pump-action screwdriver works by converting downward movement of the sliding handle into rotation of the tip. So, simply by pushing hard, the screw is driven very quickly in or out of the wood (depending on the setting of the ratchet).

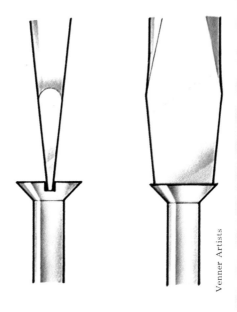

**B.** *Always ensure that the blade of your screwdriver fits the screw head exactly and that the tip is kept ground square. If you do not, you will risk damaging the workpiece or chewing up the screw slot*

When using a pump-action screwdriver, hold it firmly in both hands— one on the handle, the other on the knurled collar just above the bit— and make sure that you are not off-balance (fig 10). A sudden loss of control causes the blade to slip out of its screw slot—damaging your wood in the process.

To make screwdriving easier, the screws can be lubricated with wax or candle grease before driving. Brass screws are quite soft and to prevent damage when screwing into hardwood, the resistance can be lowered by driving in a harder steel screw of the same size first.

*Nigel MacIntyre / Wallpaper courtesy of Sanderson Ltd.*

# Build a bunk bed

### Cutting list
The list quotes finished lengths timber. Add on at least 15mm each length to allow for accura cuts 'on the waste side of the line

**Legs:** 4 No. 50mm x 50m x 1480mm

**Side rails:** 4 No. 100mm x 25m x 2065mm; 2 No. 100mm x 25m x 708mm; 2 No. 50mm x 25m x 708mm

**End rails:** 8 No. 100mm x 25m x 760mm; 4 No. 50mm x 25m x 760mm; 2 No. 75mm x 25m x 760mm

**Base support rails:** 4 No. 50m x 25mm x 716mm; 4 No. 50m x 25mm x 1921mm

**Outer ladder stiles:** 2 No. 50m x 25mm x 1250mm

**Inner ladder stiles:** 2 No. 50m x 22mm x 1950mm

**Plywood leaves:** 2 No. 760m x 1921mm x 9mm

**Ladder rungs:** 3 No. 25m chromed steel tube x 649mm

Use 32mm No. 8 countersunk woo screws and white PVA adhesive c the frame: on the bed rails, use th covered type (page 75). Use 25m No. 6 screws on the bed bases

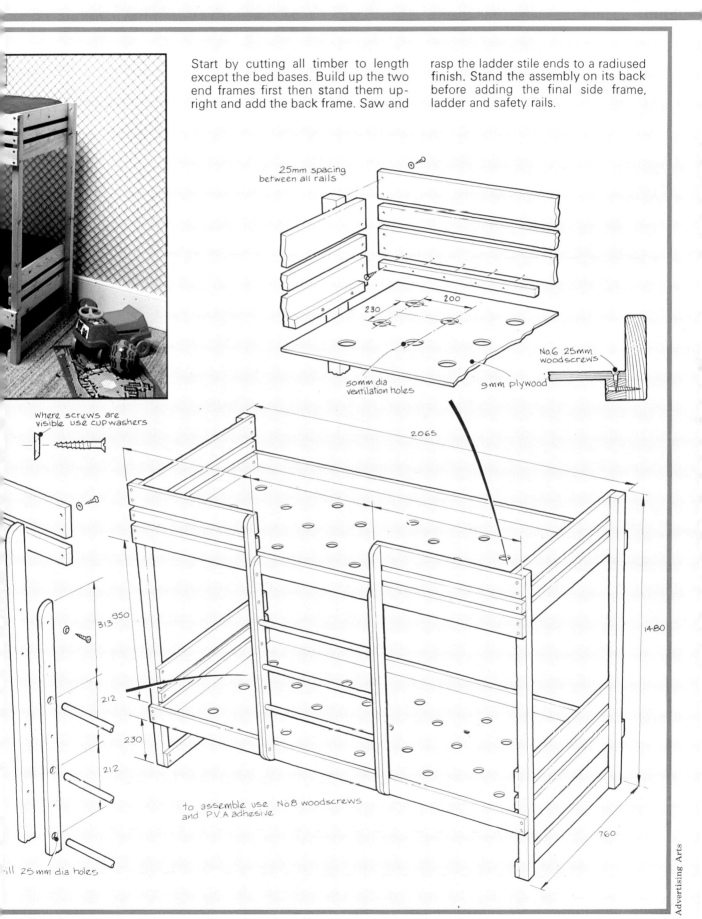

Start by cutting all timber to length except the bed bases. Build up the two end frames first then stand them upright and add the back frame. Saw and rasp the ladder stile ends to a radiused finish. Stand the assembly on its back before adding the final side frame, ladder and safety rails.

25mm spacing between all rails

230

200

50mm dia ventilation holes

9mm plywood

No.6 25mm woodscrews

2065

where screws are visible use cup washers

313 950

212

230

212

to assemble use No8 woodscrews and P.V.A adhesive

ill 25mm dia holes

1480

760

Advertising Arts

# Simple sofa

Nigel MacIntyre

**A sofa can be an expensive investment these days so making your own can save a great deal of cash. A simple frame and foam filled cushions are all you need for a basic, but comfortable sofa**

The basis of the sofa is a set of two square soft wood frames which support the backrest and bottom panel over which the upholstery hangs.

The upholstery is in two distinct parts each of which covers half the length of the sofa and provides one side rest. The foam filled panels which make up each of these separate halves are joined together at their seams with piping and the whole arrangement is simply thrown over the frame and ruffled into position.

A foam filled panel attached to the top of the back cushion hangs over the back and prevents the cushions from sliding around.

Since the upholstery is so easy to sew together you can completely change the appearance of your sofa simply by making several sets of cushions from differing materials and changing things around as the fancy takes you.

You can paint or stain the wood frame to suit the rest of the upholst and the decor of your living room, a natural wood finish will blend w just about any type of cushion cov ing from hessian to felt or corduroy

The open plan wooden support fra allows easy access underneath the s for cleaning and the whole thing is light it can easily be moved around any member of the family.

You can make matching cha simply by reducing the overall leng of the sofa, so you can build up a th or even four or five piece suite as y go along.

Maintenance and cleaning could be simpler as all the upholstery instantly removable.

# Workplan

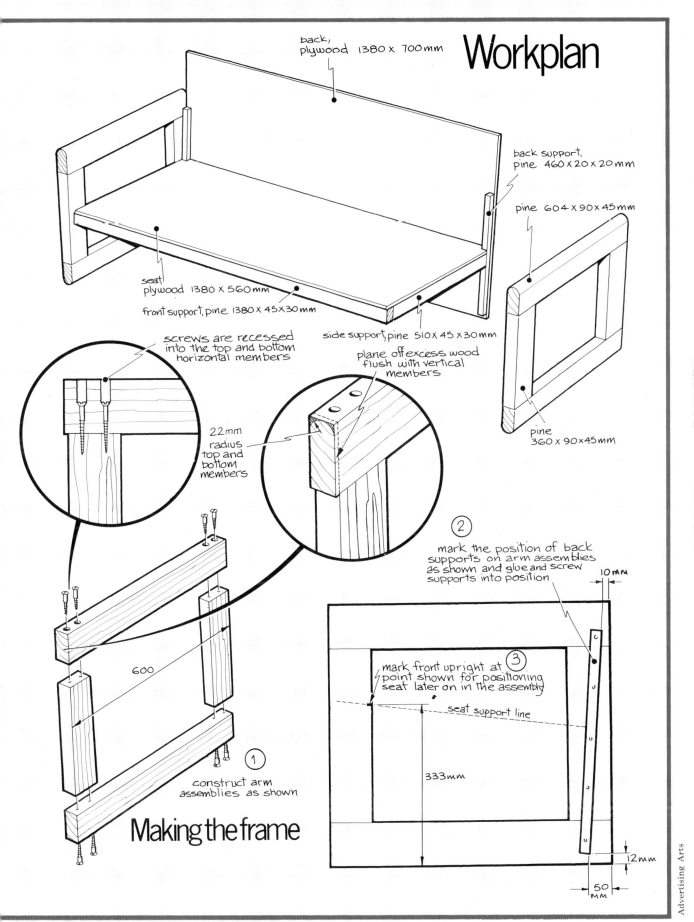

back, plywood 1380 x 700mm

back support, pine 460 x 20 x 20mm

pine 604 x 90 x 45mm

seat, plywood 1380 x 560mm

front support, pine 1380 x 45 x 30mm

side support, pine 510 x 45 x 30mm

pine 360 x 90 x 45mm

screws are recessed into the top and bottom horizontal members

plane off excess wood flush with vertical members

22mm radius top and bottom members

600

① construct arm assemblies as shown

## Making the frame

② mark the position of back supports on arm assemblies as shown and glue and screw supports into position

10mm

mark front upright at point shown for positioning seat later on in the assembly

③

seat support line

333mm

12mm

50 mm

# Project

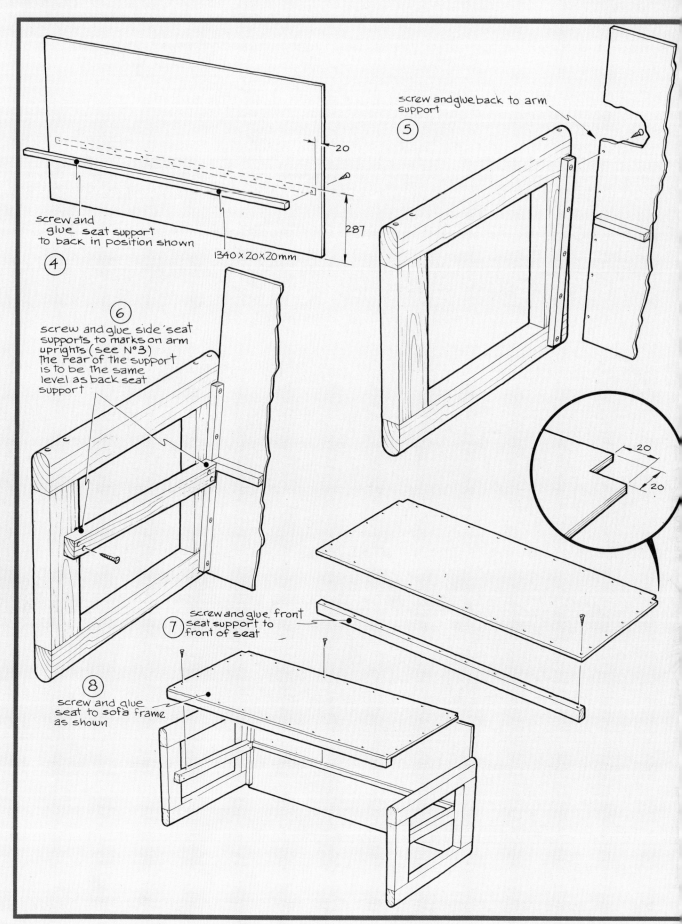

screw and
glue seat support
to back in position shown

④

1340 x 20 x 20mm

287

20

screw and glue back to arm
support

⑤

⑥
screw and glue side seat
supports to marks on arm
uprights (see N°3)
the rear of the support
is to be the same
level as back seat
support

20

20

screw and glue front
⑦ seat support to
front of seat

⑧
screw and glue
seat to sofa frame
as shown

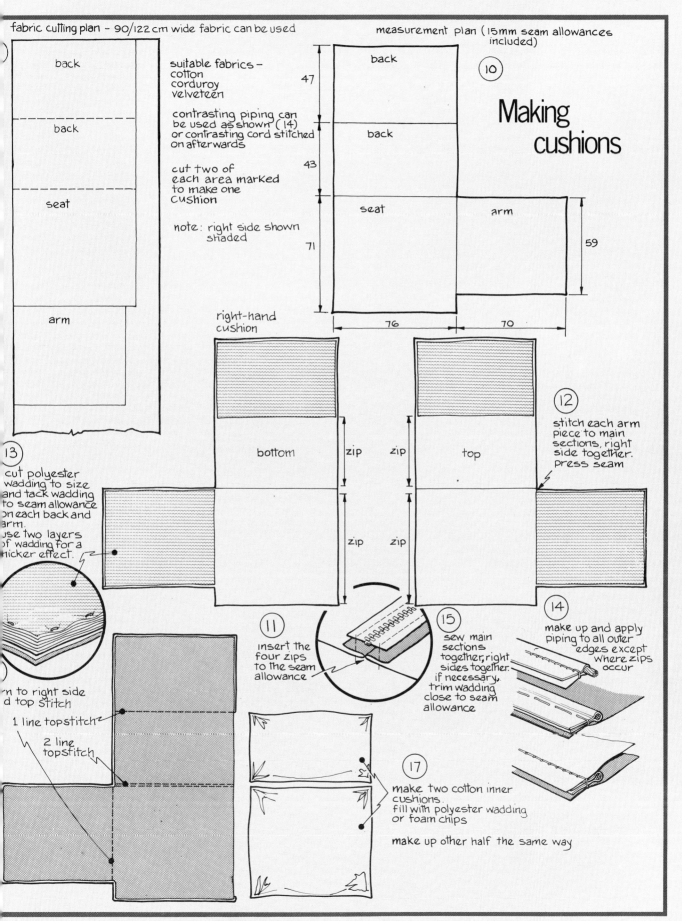

fabric cutting plan - 90/122 cm wide fabric can be used

back

back

seat

arm

suitable fabrics –
cotton
corduroy
velveteen

contrasting piping can
be used as shown (14)
or contrasting cord stitched
on afterwards

cut two of
each area marked
to make one
cushion

note: right side shown
shaded

measurement plan (15mm seam allowances
included)

back

47

back

43

seat        arm

71        59

76        70

⑩

# Making
# cushions

right-hand
cushion

⑬ cut polyester
wadding to size
and tack wadding
to seam allowance
on each back and
arm.
use two layers
of wadding for a
thicker effect.

bottom        zip        zip        top

zip        zip

⑫ stitch each arm
piece to main
sections, right
side together.
press seam

⑪ insert the
four zips
to the seam
allowance

⑮ sew main
sections
together, right
sides together.
if necessary,
trim wadding
close to seam
allowance

⑭ make up and apply
piping to all outer
edges except
where zips
occur

...rn to right side
..d top stitch

1 line topstitch

2 line
topstitch

⑰ make two cotton inner
cushions.
fill with polyester wadding
or foam chips

make up other half the same way

81

# Wallpaper without fuss

**Preparing the walls ● Stripping wallpaper
The right tools for the job ●
Matching the pattern ● Measuring and
cutting ● Pasting and folding ●
Papering around corners and sockets**

**A**. *When papering over vinyl
wallpaper, simply peel away the
outer layer. The paper below can
stay on the wall*

Wallpapering may look simple, but it
is all too easy to get into a mess unless
you know the right way to do it. Most
of the techniques involved are easily
mastered and will help give your walls
a professional touch.

### Preparing the room
Start by removing as much furniture
from the room as possible, then
remove all wall hangings—such as
pictures, mirrors and lamps—together
with their fixings.

To mark the future positions of the
fixings, stick a steel pin into each
wall-plug—later, you can hang wallpaper over the pins and leave the
fixings clearly marked. Protect the
floor with dust sheets: polythe[ne]
sheets tend to be too slippery a[nd]
paper will make a mess if it gets dam[p].

### Preparing the surface
**Painted walls:** Unless the paint [is]
flaking or the surface is uneve[n,]
painted walls do not have to [be]
stripped. However, make sure th[at]
the surfaces are completely free [of]
grease and dirt. To give the new wa[ll]
paper something to grip on—espe[ci]
ally if the surface is gloss—block-sa[nd]
the surface and wipe clean.
**Bare walls:** Freshly plastered [or]
rendered walls and walls that ha[ve]
been stripped to the plaster can [be]
papered over with little trouble, p[ro]
viding they are free of damp. Yo[ur]
first task is to make good any ch[ips]
or cracks in the surface with fil[ler]
and to sand down bumps and bulg[es].

For the small blemishes norma[lly]
encountered when redecorating, u[se]
either a cellulose-based filler in po[w]
der form (such as Polyfilla), or [a]
ready-mixed vinyl-based compou[nd]
which comes in tubs.

Cellulose fillers are the cheaper [of]
the two and are suitable for m[ost]
internal uses, but the hard-dryi[ng]
qualities of vinyl-based fillers come [in]
handy where the cracks result fr[om]
expansion due to heat—around h[ot]
water pipes for instance.

The secret of using filler is to app[ly]
a little at a time, waiting for ea[ch]
layer to dry before you apply the ne[xt].
In the case of powder fillers, m[ix]
enough for just one layer at a time[—]
an old tennis ball cut in half make[s a]
good container.

efore you apply any of the filler, sh away all loose debris from und the hole and blow away any t. Use a flexible filling knife or old kitchen palette knife to force first layer well into the hole. ile it is drying, clean the knife and pe away any excess filler from the face of the wall.

Continue building up the filler until is just proud, then smooth it off h the knife. When the filler is dry, fine glass paper on a cork sanding ck to sand it—and any other nps—flush with the wall.

Sizing or painting the wall with a table compound, evens out the orbent qualities of the plaster or der and creates a smooth surface which to wallpaper. If you are

Soaking and scraping tends to be a messy job and if just water is used to soften the paper it can also be hard work. So where medium and heavy-weight papers are concerned, you can add either proprietary stripping compound or some vinegar or acetic acid —available from chemists—to the water. All these reduce the surface tension of the water, helping it soak into the paper more quickly and break down the old paste.

Normally, the mix is simply painted on with a distemper brush. But if you are dealing with PVA-coated washable paper, you may need to score the surface with a wire brush so that the stripper can penetrate through to the wall. Leave the stripper to soak for a few minutes, then use a stripping

off the loosened paper with the other. These operations soon become continuous with practice, although the thick layers of paper may require more than one application.

## Preparing to paper

A good working surface on which to cut and paste the wallpaper is essential. Ideally, you should use a pasting board about 25mm narrower than the paper you are hanging. Alternatively, use a sheet of chipboard or a flush-faced door—laid over a pair of trestles or the kitchen table. To help you reach the top of the walls, you will also need at least one pair of steps. Make sure that these are safe.

Arrange the equipment so that you can work on it comfortably and

*A steam stripping machine makes light work of stripping avier papers. Easy to use, they can obtained from most hire shops*

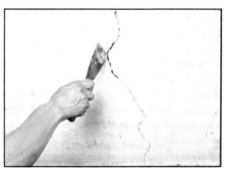

**2** *Taking the trouble to fill cracks in the wall before you paper over it will improve the overall finish. Build up the filler in layers*

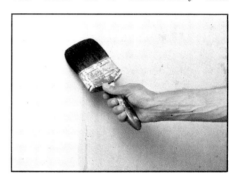

**3** *Sizing a plastered wall before you paper over it will stop the paste from soaking in too quickly and causing the paper to peel later*

ng a cellulose wallpaper paste below), use this as your sizing pound. For starch pastes a bone size is available. Vinyl wallpaper tes require their own, special size. ve the wall to dry thoroughly re you start hanging your paper.

lls already papered: In most es, it is inadvisable to lay fresh er over an already papered wall— r-papering causes the paste bet-n layers to interact, giving rise to itional problems such as peeling, ning and blistering.

lowever, with vinyl-laminated er, it is sometimes possible to l away the vinyl layer from its er backing strip. If the backing er remains firmly and evenly ted to the wall, you can paper ectly on to it.

## ipping wallpaper

re are two methods of stripping lpaper in general use: soaking and ping—with or without a proprie-y stripping compound—and steam-pping, using a special tool.

knife to scrape it away from the wall. Make sure that your knife is kept ground sharp. Ideally, it should be of the type which has a stiff steel blade incorporated into the handle—the cheaper varieties bend and gouge plaster out of the wall.

If a piece of paper proves particularly stubborn, paint on some more water, leave it to soak, then try again—on no account attack a stubborn patch with the scraper as you may damage the plaster. Like washable paper, thick layers of old paper can be shifted more quickly if you carefully score the surface first with a wire brush.

Steam stripping is about as fast as using water but requires much less effort, creates less mess and minimizes the chances of damaging the wall. You can hire a steam stripper quite cheaply from hire shops and, if your old wallpaper is particularly heavy, it is worth the cost.

To use the tool, you simply press the steam-generating pad against the wall with one hand (fig 1) and scrape

safely, not forgetting that you will often need both hands free to hang the wallpaper. At the same time, gather together all the other tools necessary for the job—plumbline, shears, tape measure, pasting brush, pencil and bucket. The shears are particularly important—try not to economize by using ordinary household scissors which are too small for accurate cuts on this scale.

One final preparatory step is to compare the shades of each separate roll of wallpaper. Where the batch numbers on the outer packing are the same, there should be no problem. But if the numbers differ, check the colour of each roll and arrange them so that similar shades run next to each other when you come to paste them up on the wall.

## Where to start

Where you start papering depends to a large extent on whether your wallpaper is subdued, or bold and striking. In the former case, follow the general rule that you should always paper

# Decorating 2

**4** To mark up the wall for the first strip, measure the width of your roll along the wall from your chosen starting point and make a mark

**5** Next, to give some overlap at the starting point, measure back 25mm from the mark. Repeat this procedure at the base of the wall

Secure a plumbline running fr
the top of the wall and through t
point, rub it with chalk, then sr
it against the wall as shown in fig
This leaves a vertical chalk line do
the wall which in turn acts as a gu
to help you position the side edge
the first strip.

Slide the paper upwards until ab
25mm overlaps the top of the w
with the sides flush against the ch
line, then crease it along the junct
with the ceiling. Still holding it
position, crease the bottom of
strip in the same way.

Although you will be trimming e
strip, it is still a good idea to
them square. So, having marked y
first strip, lay the paper out on
table and cut across the strip 35
from the bottom crease.

When measuring the next st
use the edge of the first as a gui
Allow an overlap for trimming top
bottom, then mark and cut it as
cribed above. If your wallpaper
patterned, make sure that you ma
the design from strip to strip—bef
you allow for your top overlap.

Wallpapers with patterns wh
match on each horizontal line can
matched in strips without difficu
But if you find that you have to al

**6** You can now fix a plumbline in line with the two marks. Having chalked the line and secured it on the wall, snap it back

**7** Align your first strip of wall-paper against the chalk mark. Do not forget to allow for an overlap top and bottom

away from the light—any overlaps between strips will cast shadows if you make them facing into it.

Start at the end of a wall, or against a window or door frame—where you will have a straight run before tackling the more intricate bits.

Where the wallpaper you have chosen has a bold pattern, start with a feature wall or chimney breast which immediately catches the eye. Centre up the pattern so it is symmetrical then work on from either side.

If your wallpaper pattern consists of strong geometric shapes, plan for the final strip to be hung in an obscure corner of the room—well away from the light—where the break in pattern is not too noticeable.

## Measuring and cutting

The simplest way of measuring and cutting wallpaper is to offer each strip up to the wall as you go along. But use a plumbline to make sure that the first strip is straight or you will run into difficulties later on.

Having chosen your starting point, which should be in a corner or against a door frame, measure from this along the top of the wall 25mm less than the width of your roll and mark the spot with a pencil.

**8** When you are cutting strips of wallpaper, take the overlap on to match the pattern. Fold the paper back on itself to keep the cut square

**9** When pasting a strip, paste the edges of the strip off the table. This will avoid accidentally getting paste on the other side of the pape

**10** Folding strips 'paste to paste' as shown makes them far easier to handle. The end you paste last will go at the top of the wall

**11** Cutting strips lengthways is easier if you paste and fold them first. Mark cutting lines in pencil and slice them with the she

overlap of about half a strip's
[len]gth before the pattern matches,
[you] have what is known as a 'half
[dro]p and repeat' pattern.

[I]n this case, save on wallpaper by
[wor]king with two rolls at a time. Take
[you]r first strip from the first roll,
[you]r second strip from the second
[rol]l, and so on.

[A]t the end of the first wall, you
[wil]l almost certainly have to cut a
[stri]p lengthways to get it to fit. Do
[thi]s when the strip has been pasted
[and] folded. Measure the width of the
[gap] top and bottom, transfer this to
[the] whole strip then mark the strip
[off] with a straight edge. Cut down
[this] line with the shears (fig 11).

### [Pa]sting and folding

[Wh]en pasting wallpaper it is impor-
[tan]t to stop the paste from getting on
[the] table (fig 9). Note that edges
[are] only pasted when they overhang
[the] table. Brush on the paste in a
[cro]ss-cross 'herringbone' fashion, en-
[sur]ing not only an even coverage but
[als]o that the edges receive plenty of
[pas]te. Work from the middle of the
[stri]p outwards.

[W]hen you have paste about two-
[thi]rds of the strip, take the top edge
[in] your fingers and thumbs and fold
[the] strip down on itself. Make sure
[tha]t the edges line up then slide the
[res]t of the strip on to the table and
[pas]te it. Fold this back on itself as
[wel]l, so that you are left with two
[fol]ds—a large one at the top of the
[str]ip and a small one at the bottom of
[the] strip (fig 10).

[I]f your strips of wallpaper are
[par]ticularly large, you may find that
[you] will have to increase the size of
[the] bottom fold. Short strips need be
[fol]ded only once.

[R]eady pasted paper must be soaked
[in] water before hanging in order to
[act]ivate the adhesive on the back.
[Ha]ving cut a strip to length and folded
[to] fit your water tray, immerse it for
[abo]ut a minute and move the tray to
[dir]ectly below the wall to be papered.
[Yo]u can then lift the strip straight out
[of] the tray and on to the wall. Smooth
[and] trim it as you would ordinary
[pap]er with the shears.

### [Ha]nging and trimming

[Li]ft the folded strip off the pasting
[tab]le, take the top edge in your
[fin]gers and thumbs and allow the top
[fol]d to drop. Lay the strip against
[the] wall, in line with your chalk line
[at] the side and with the crease
[mar]king the trimming overlap at the
[top]. Brush down the middle of the

strip with the paperhanger's brush
and unfurl the bottom fold.

Next, lightly press down the edges
to be trimmed. Mark off the waste by
running along the creases with the
back of your shears, then pull the
edges away from the wall again.

Cut along each crease mark in turn,
pressing the finished edges down as
you go. Run over the finished job
with the brush to remove air bubbles
—working from the centre of the
strip out towards the edges and using
short, light, strokes.

Butt subsequent strips up against
each other so the side edges touch,
but do not overlap. Make sure that
the pattern matches at the top of the
wall before you start trimming, or you
waste much paper.

### Switches and sockets

First offer up the pasted strip in the
normal way, lining it up with your
plumbed line or an adjacent strip.
Brush the top part of the strip down
against the wall to hold it in place,
but leave the rest of the paper hanging freely over the obstruction.

Now press the strip lightly over the
obstruction so that its outline is left
indented on the paper. Pull the strip
out from the wall again and pierce it
with the shears, roughly in the
middle of the indentations. Gently
snip out to the four corners of the
indented mark so you are left with
four triangular flaps (fig 13).

In the case of a round switch, pierce
the centre of the circle and make
several radial cuts out towards the
edge. Trim the flaps away with a
sharp knife, wiping off excess paste
as you go (fig 14).

### Papering around corners

When you come to an internal corner,
follow the rule of papering in with one
piece and out again with another.
As you paper in allow about 25mm

**12** *When you have positioned a strip correctly on the wall, crease the overlaps, peel away the paper around them and trim*

**13** *Where the paper goes over a switch or socket, crease an impression of the outline then make vee-shaped cuts to the corners*

**14** *Trim away the flaps with a sharp knife. On circular switches, use the same procedure but make more cuts to the edges*

**15** *When you are measuring thin strips before corners, do not forget to take measurements at both the top and bottom of the wall*

**16** *Butt a strip before a corner up against the previous strip, then crease the overlap into the corner with the back of your shears*

overlap and crease the paper into the corner with the back of the shears.

Whenever you paper out, plumb a fresh line on the adjoining wall first. As you hang the paper, align it with the plumbed line and make sure it goes well into the corner to cover the overlap on the previous strip.

Folding paper around an external corner will only be possible if the corner is vertical and cleanly finished.

If you have any doubts, treat the corner as you would an internal one.

Paper up to it with your first piece, allow an overlap of 25mm and fold this around corner. Having plumbed a fresh line, hang your second strip, again allowing about 25mm over the corner for trimming. Make sure that the second strip is firmly stuck to the overlap of the first, then trim it flush with the edge of the corner.

**17** *Always plumb a fresh line before turning a corner. As you hang the next strip, run the overlap into the corner, crease and trim it*

**18** *On small sections of wall, there is no need to plumb a line. Align one side of the strip on the edge with the other overlapping*

## Papering a window reveal

**Top right:** *When papering into a window reveal or bay window, cut your first strip so that you can fold part of it round as shown.*
**Below:** *Continue laying strips across the wall around the reveal. Leave the ends of the shorter strips hanging at this stage.*
**Below right:** *Paper the top of the reveal, leaving enough overlap to turn each strip up on to the wall. Finally, stick the hanging ends down and trim them to length. Paper the remaining parts in the normal way*

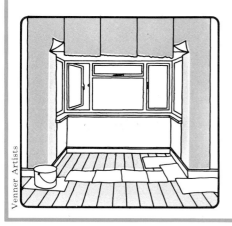

Venner Artists

# Ideas for wallpaper borders

Used on their own, wallpa[...] borders add a touch of style a[...] elegance to a plain painted room[...]

Available from most wallpa[...] and decorating shops, they [...] normally employed to finish of[...] semi-papered wall which has [...] picture rail. But the borders [...] often be used to better effect[...] highlight windows and alcov[...] pick out fixed wall mirrors [...] extend architraves and covings.

The borders are pasted up in [...] same way as ordinary wallpaper[...] is a good idea though, to penci[...] the positions of the strips so t[...] you can make alterations bef[...] they are stuck down.

To make the mitred (angl[...] joints between strips, cut th[...] overlength so that they overlap [...] another. When you paste them [...] put a piece of paper between [...] flaps then cut through the strips[...] the desired angle.

# On a firm footing

**All about concrete ● Calculating quantities ● Working out the size of your foundations ● Mixing your own concrete ● Setting out and digging a trench ● Levelling off**

Most modern constructions stand on foundations made from concrete. Such foundations are necessary for three reasons. They spread a structure's load over an area large enough to prevent undue settlement occurring. They bridge over any soft spots which may exist in the ground. And they provide a level base for the structure.

### Simple foundations

Although foundations vary enormously in complexity, those used for garden projects—walls, barbecues and planters—can be of the simple, strip type. Also known as footings, these are made by digging a trench

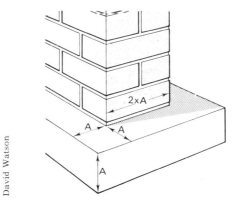

**A.** *Use this diagram to calculate the width and depth of your foundations*

**1** *Your stakes and marker lines need only stay in for as long as it takes to dig out an impression of the length and width of the trench*

**2** *As you dig the trench, make sure that the sides and floor are as straight and as level as possible. Remove dug soil immediately*

**3** *The pegs indicating the depth your foundations should be driven into the floor of the trench, about 1m apart, then levelled off*

and then pouring in a measured amount of concrete.

Concrete paths and the slabs on which greenhouses and garden sheds rest come under the classification of raft foundations. These are made with the aid of pieces of timber—formwork—laid out before the concrete is poured to give the finished slab a uniform shape. Raft foundations are covered in detail further on in the course.

### Concrete

Concrete is a mixture of Portland cement, aggregate and water. Aggregate is made from sand, stones, or

some other inactive material and is supplied in fine, coarse, or mixed varieties. Mixed aggregate is often called *all-in ballast*: since it is a mixture of sand and stones it is easily hand mixed and is suitable for all kinds of amateur projects.

When first mixed, concrete consists of particles of stone and sand bound together by a paste of cement and water. As the paste dries it hardens—bonding the stones into a strong, durable structure.

This process takes place in less than a couple of hours so time is always an important factor when you are working with concrete.

### Which mix to use

The composition of a batch of concrete is expressed in the building trade as a ratio of cement to sand shingle, in that order. So if a mix described as 1:3:6, it means volume of cement and three of sand six volumes of shingle.

At the builders' merchants, however, the sand and gravel is normally sold mixed as all-in ballast. simple foundations, ask for '18mm ballast'. The 18mm means there no particles in the mix bigger than 18mm across and 1:6 means that you need six volumes of ballast to one cement for each batch.

**4** *Having mixed the dry ingredients form a crater in the middle of the heap then pour in your measured quantity of water*

**5** *Turn over the mixture until it reaches the consistency shown here. Puddles in the mix mean you have added too much water*

**B. Left:** *Concrete is a versatile material, ideal for all sorts of small garden projects*

**C. Below left:** *The correct way to set out simple footings, leaving out the structure lines*

The strength of a batch of concrete also depends on its water content at the time of mixing and laying so it is important to make sure that the correct amount of water is used. For a 1:6 cement to ballast mix, use about two volumes of water.

### Calculating quantities
For simple footings, there is no need to involve yourself in the complex calculations used in housebuilding. Use the diagram in fig. A to calculate the length, width and depth of the footing then multiply the figures together to find the volume of concrete required. Add on a little extra to the result—it is better to have too much concrete than to have to buy more half way through the job.

The method shown in fig. A will be enough to satisfy the Building Regulations on small projects only. Do not attempt to use it for structural work—such as house extensions—where strict guidelines on the size of foundation and mix of concrete you can use come into force.

If you are planning to build on particularly soft soil, you may need to reinforce your foundation trench with a little hardcore before you pour in the concrete. Your local building inspector can advise on this.

### Readymix or do-it-yourself?
The ingredients for concrete can either be bought unmixed from a

builders' merchant or delivered by truck, readymixed. The latter saves a great deal of hard work but will probably be too expensive for small projects using less than 2.5m³ of concrete. You may also have difficulty persuading the concrete company to deliver such a small load.

If you decide on ready-mixed concrete, bear in mind that it must be laid and levelled within two hours of delivery and that the truck will need access to the site.

One of the advantages of mixing your own concrete is that you can do the job in stages, mixing just enough for your needs. If the concreting is extensive, consider hiring a small mixer. Make sure, though, that you have it fully demonstrated before leaving the hire shop.

### Mixing your own concrete
To hand mix concrete, measure out bucketfuls of sand and gravel—or all-in ballast—and arrange them in a large heap on-site. Each bucketful should correspond to one 'volume' of your mix. Hollow out a crater in the top of the heap and add a measured volume of cement.

Turn over the mixture three or four times until it is uniformly coloured—with no cement streaks—then re-form it into a volcano shape.

Now pour in some of your measured volumes of water—not from the same bucket as the cement—and shovel up the dry ingredients from the bottom of the heap (fig 4). Turn the mixture over again, adding more water as you go, until a firm, even paste is formed.

To check if a batch has been correctly mixed, press hard on it with the back of the trowel or the heel of your boot. The impression you make

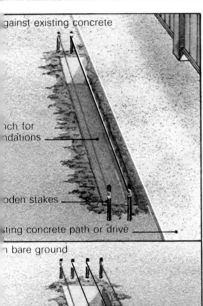

against existing concrete

ch for
ndations

oden stakes

sting concrete path or drive

n bare ground

nch

oden stakes

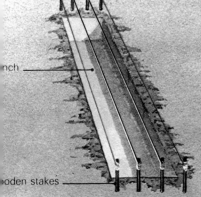

— nylon line marking edge of foundation trench

— nylon line marking one side of brick structure to be built

**6** *Use a bucket to transport the mix to where it is needed. Carrying it on a shovel takes too long and may make a mess of the site*

**7** *Before you pour the mix into the trench, remember to drive marker pegs in to indicate the foundations' depth. The peg tops should be level*

**8** *Shovel each bucketful of concrete as shown to ensure that it fills out the trench complete and comes up to the level of the pe*

should have a firm, closed surface free of water patches, pits and lumps.

## Setting out

For setting out simple footings, you need a couple of sets of bricklayers' line and a supply of wooden pegs half as long again as the depth of the concrete. You can use nylon fishing line instead of bricklayers' line—but not string, which will stretch and sag. Make the pegs from wood offcuts.

The lines are used to indicate the widths of both the foundation trench and the structure above. If you are building flush against a concrete drive or path, only two lines are needed: one to indicate the other boundary of the foundations and one to mark the main wall of your structure.

Having decided on your site, measure it out and score the boundaries with a spade. At either end, drive in stakes to mark the widths of the foundation trench and the structure to be built on it (fig C).

Connect the stakes with your line, tied taught so that you have an arrangement similar to that shown in fig C. Keep the lines as far up the stakes as possible so that you have room to dig underneath them.

Where the ground is soft enough, you may find it easier to score out the sides of the trench then remove the stakes and lines before you start digging. To do this, hold a spirit level on end, plumb against each line and mark off the ground at regular intervals. Join up the marks with the edge or your spade.

Otherwise, use the lines as a digging guide. Try not to disturb the ground any more than is necessary—simply dig down to the required depth of the foundations, keeping the floor of the trench as flat as possible.

**9** *Checking with straight edge between peg tops shows up any unevenness. This can be put right by adding or removing concrete*

With the trench dug, the next step is to drive your wooden pegs into the floor. These will stay in place when the concrete is poured, indicating the final level of the foundations.

Start at one end of the trench, driving your first peg in until it protrudes to the required depth of concrete (fig 1). Drive in subsequent pegs at intervals of about 1m. Using a spirit level, check each peg with the preceding one to ensure that they are all exactly horizontal.

## Pouring the concrete

Concreting should begin at the furthest point from where the concrete is being mixed. Avoid forceably throwing the concrete in to the trench as this causes the larger particles of ballast to separate from the mix.

Fill the trench up to the level of your marker pegs. If the foundations are to be particularly deep, pour in concrete to a depth of about 200mm then flatten it out with a piece of timber before you add more.

**10** *When the concrete is as leve, as you can get it, lightly run over the surface with a piece of wood in a 'chopping' motion*

When you reach the stage whe the concrete looks more or less le with all the pegs, begin levelling Use the edge of a piece of timber flatten the surface (fig 10). Do this a 'chopping' motion, moving the ti ber along about 50mm each time.

Finally, test the overall level of t concrete by resting a straight edge spirit level on each marker peg in tu Remove any excess concrete and level where necessary.

## Drying

At this point, the footings are co plete and ready to be left to d Although they should be ready build on the following day, the m drying time you can allow the bett

In hot weather, moisten the surf of the setting concrete regularly w a watering can. This will stop it s ting prematurely and cracking. conditions of extreme cold are exp ted, place some hay or old packag material over the concrete to insul it, then cover it with plastic sheet.

# An attractive stepped planter

This stepped planter project adds an attractive focal point to any garden. The design is based upon the simplest of all bonds—the stretcher bond—but uses half-bricks all the way along the top course.

The ground in front of the planter can be covered with two concrete slabs, laid on a base of tamped (compressed) hardcore topped with mortar. Alternatively, you can leave it as bare soil or grass.

½ bats as soldiers

slab

**100mm concrete** — **slab laid on 1:8 lime sand over 100mm tamped hardcore**

The foundations for the planter are shown overleaf. Build them using a 1:6 cement/ballast mix to the dimensions given. For the structure, you need 265 bricks plus an allowance for breakages. 45 of the bricks are cut in half and stood on end as 'soldiers' to finish off the top courses. For the mortar, allow 1 50kg bag of cement and 4 50kg bags of sand. The optional concrete slabs measure 915mm x 610mm and rest on a bed of mortar laid over 100mm of tamped hardcore.

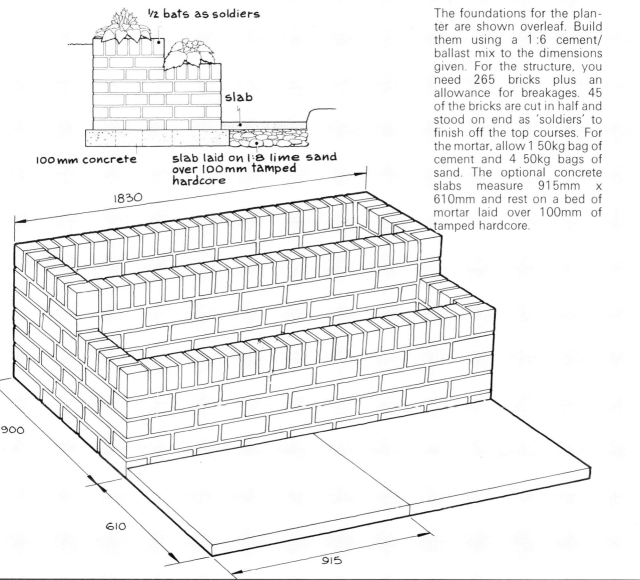

1830
900
610
915

# Course layout

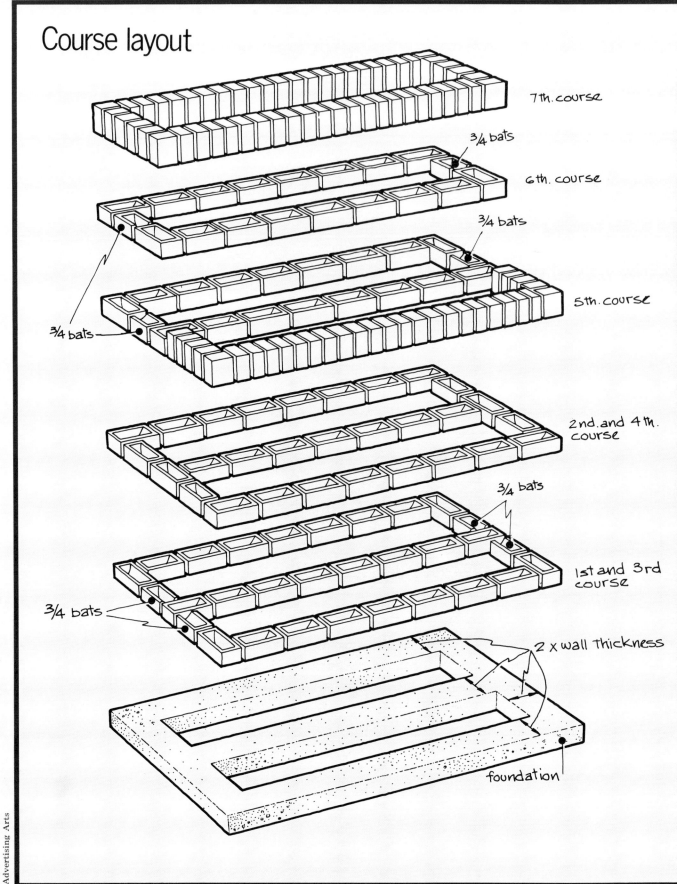

7th. course

3/4 bats

6th. course

3/4 bats

3/4 bats

5th. course

2nd. and 4th. course

3/4 bats

1st and 3rd course

3/4 bats

2 x wall thickness

foundation

# Plan your kitchen

well planned kitchen should be easy to use,
asy to clean and still be a pleasant place in
hich to work. Even the smallest kitchens can
eet all these requirements

**Below**: *A U-shaped kitchen which
has all the essential kitchen
equipment and an enviable amount of
worktop space—and every area is
well-lit. Display storage adds a
homely touch*

Elizabeth Whiting

en if you have a small kitchen,
reful planning, a little reorgani-
tion and a fair amount of impro-
sation can transform it into an
icient and pleasant place to be.

Studies have shown that in most
tchens, the activity centres around
ree main areas—those of food stor-
e (pantry and fridge), the sink and
e stove. From this information, the
ea of an ideal work triangle has
olved: this forms the basis of
tchen planning no matter what the
ze of your kitchen.

The corners of the triangle are
eally linked by work surfaces, pro-
ding areas for food preparation,
xing and serving. The perfect work
angle keeps distances between the

sink, fridge and cooker as short as
possible. Ideally, a trip around it
should measure between 3.5m and 7m.

## Making a plan of the layout

The best way of planning a kitchen is
to draw up a scale plan of the layout
on graph paper. You can use any scale
you like—although 1/25, where each
5mm square of graph paper represents
100mm of kitchen, is normally the
most convenient.

Start by drawing the basic outline.
Mark on it all fixed objects—the
radiators, power points, chimney
breast, alcoves—and also the swing
of doors and windows.

Next, on a separate sheet of graph
paper and to the same scale as your

outline, draw up the outlines of your
chosen units and appliances. Having
labelled them for easy identification,
cut out the shapes and transfer them
to your outline plan. Juggle them
around on the graph until you have
a sensible, practical arrangement.

When positioning appliances, start
with the sink: unless you want to be
bothered with the lengthy and sometimes expensive process of moving it,
it is best left where it is.

A small sink with only one drainer
is best for a small kitchen and where
space is really limited, consider doing
without a drainer altogether. Use a
draining rack instead, standing it on
the window ledge or screwing it to the
wall. If the rack is of the decorative

93

# Home designer

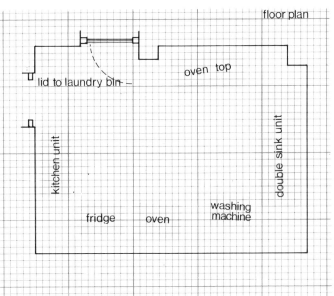

floor plan

lid to laundry bin —

oven top

kitchen unit

double sink unit

fridge     oven     washing machine

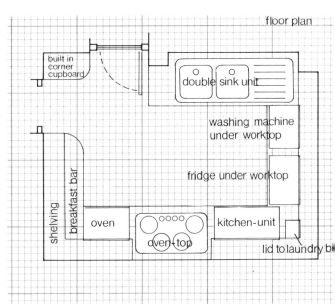

floor plan

built in corner cupboard

double sink unit

washing machine under worktop

fridge under worktop

shelving

breakfast bar

oven     oven top     kitchen-unit

lid to laundry bin

**Above**: *Use coloured shapes to the same scale as your plan to represent all the units and equipment. Move them around until you have the most practical arrangement* (**above right**)

**Right**: *A kitchen with an ideal working layout. Valuable space is saved by placing the plate racks above the sink instead of on a separate drainer*

wooden kind, it can act as a display area that also saves on cupboard space elsewhere.

By making a wall plan as well as a floor one, you will have a more comprehensive idea of the space available. Before you make plans for your walls, however, check what they are made of—a partition made of plasterboard, for example, is no place to hang a heavy wall cupboard.

If you have an expanse of wall, measuring around 3m, you can have what is considered the ideal kitchen layout of worksurface, sink, worksurface, cooker, worksurface, Otherwise, the three most common kitchen layouts are the galley, L-shaped and U-shaped. The ideal triangle can be incorporated into all of them.

## Useful measurements

The average height of manufactured units is between 950mm and 975mm—the most comfortable height for the average woman of 1.6m. However, if for some reason you want a different height, you can either make your own units or buy a system which is adjustable for height.

If possible, the width of the gangway in a galley-type kitchen should be not less than 1200mm. This allows ough space for one person to bend own to a cupboard and for another to ve past at the same time without much of a squeeze.

The average-sized adult has diffi-ty reaching higher than 1520mm so to store items which are used ularly at this height. Where there no worksurface to lean over, the ght of the shelf or cupboard can be sed a little. Site wall cupboards at st 400mm above the work surface or y will obscure the back of it.

or sitting on high stools, the ommended space underneath a rksurface is 460mm. This space is o sufficient for storing the stool so u are not repeatedly tripping over it. e stool should be low enough to give ee space of around 150mm under-ath the worktop.

The worktop should project at least

Consider, also, what you want out of the kitchen. Decide whether your worksurfaces will all be required for food preparation, or whether some of the space can be used for eating or for display purposes.

With a small kitchen you may have to make some compromises, although there is no reason why it should not still function as well. As far as appliances are concerned, it is worth shopping around for these, not only because you may get a bargain, but also because you may find smaller versions fairly easily.

Upright, four-burner gas stoves and plug-in, electric stovettes with a two

**Right:** *A sophisticated example of how tiles can be used effectively on all kitchen surfaces, including the frames of the units*

Elizabeth Whiting

U-shaped kitchen

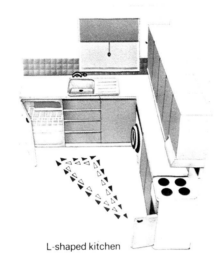

L-shaped kitchen

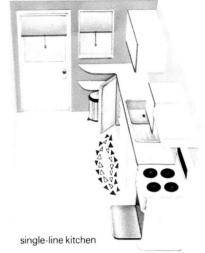

single-line kitchen

oove: *The distance between the dge, sink and cooker should be as se as possible to the ideal work angle of between 3.5m and 7m. e shape works in most kitchens*

mm beyond the unit base to allow something to be held at the edge to tch the crumbs when wiping it wn after use.

Free-standing stoves are not in-lated so you should leave an all-und gap of at least 100mm between is and the surrounding worktops. is also makes them easier to clean.

## ace-saving ideas

nall kitchen owners can learn a lot out the economic use of space by udying the insides of caravans or ats. But to make more space, you ay have to consider moving certain pliances to another part of the use—such as the washing machine the bathroom.

unit hot-plate and half-size oven are ideal space savers and ample for two people.

Half-oven stoves can stand on a formica bottle rack or cupboard, giving you extra storage space instead of an oven which is never fully util-ized. The stove top can be fitted with a hinged cover to provide another worksurface when the burners or rings are not in use.

Think about whether it would be best to have a fridge with a left-hand or right-hand opening door and try to position it so that you can open the door completely. Decide also whether your family needs call for a large fridge-freezer or a small model that will fit under the work bench. Similar space saving can be achieved by siting a dishwasher under the bench.

**Right:** *The heights of the work surfaces and cupboards should all be near these average figures*

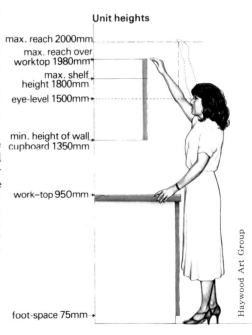

**Unit heights**

max. reach 2000mm
max. reach over worktop 1980mm
max. shelf height 1800mm
eye-level 1500mm
min. height of wall cupboard 1350mm
work-top 950mm
foot-space 75mm

Haywood Art Group

# Home designer

A front-loading automatic washing machine takes up less space than other types, but must be positioned where it can be plumbed in easily—the object is rather defeated if you have to drag the machine into the middle of the room to use it. Check, though, whether your local authority permits a clothes washing machine in the kitchen . . . quite a few do not.

If your washing machine is set at right angles to the sink unit, put a hatch on the worksurface which covers the 'dead' area and use this space for storing such things as a washing basket or shopping bags.

Shelving is probably the most versatile form of kitchen storage because it can be added to as and when you can afford a new piece of wood. Any kind of wood can be used in the kitchen as long as the brackets supporting it are good and strong.

You can use the underneath of shelves for storage jars—any old jars with metal screw-tops will do. Simply screw the lid to the underside of the shelf: you can then unscrew the jar from the lid as required. Alternatively, special storage containers are available which slot into a plastic track screwed to the bottom of the shelf.

If you have to site a heater in the kitchen and floor space is at a premium, consider opting for one of the wall-mounted types. You can also save floor space by using a waste bin which is small enough to fit in the cupboard under the sink.

Pull-out or fold-away boards, providing they are stable and solid, make space-saving alternatives to the kitchen table. The foldaway type of table, hinged to a wall bracket and matched to fold-up wooden chairs is particularly efficient.

## Storage suggestions
The whole business of designing a kitchen is easier if you are starting with an empty one. But if you have to work around other people's ideas, remember that the floor and wall cupboards can be moved to suit your needs quite easily.

If the kitchen is narrow, do not waste valuable floor space by installing units—shelves of varying widths from floor to ceiling can look really decorative and provide storage.

It is usual to site wall cupboards over the worksurfaces, but if you find it rather dismal staring at blank cupboards while working, try putting all the wall cupboards together in a batch from ceiling to floor. Remember to adjust the handles on each cupboard according to their position in the cupboard stack.

As most wall cupboards are only about 350mm deep, they do not intrude on the room yet provide plenty of storage space. This is particularly useful in a narrow kitchen which also acts as a throughway. Space-saving cupboards should have sliding, rather than hinged, doors.

Try to position floor units so that they fit right into the corners. This helps give the kitchen a really fitted look as well as providing more surface and storage space. And you should not forget to exploit your ceiling—a hanging basket makes an unusual change from the usual plastic vegetable racks.

If you do not have room for wall cupboards or shelves on your walls, a

**Above**: *A busy farmhouse look for this narrow galley kitchen—with not an inch of wasted space*

**Left**: *A fresh-looking kitchen which is both compact and practical. Note that the knives are in a safe position*

**Right**: *Ultra-modern kitchens appear less clinical with warm tiles— and good lighting is essential for all work areas*

shelf hanging from the ceiling loo most attractive. Use platicized ro through the front and back of bo ends of the shelf to support it.

Wooden garden trellis can also screwed through battens on to t ceiling and used to hang baking tra frying pans, and other utensils whi are not in daily use.

## Old made new
Imagination is what counts when y are fitting out a kitchen economical. To make this work for you, have clear idea of the style you want, th keep looking for things that fit it.

If you are tired of your existi units, try refurbishing them. Sti new laminates and handles on the do and drawer fronts—easy to do a much cheaper than buying whole ne units—and far less trouble.

Once painted and given new han les, a hotchpotch of wooden cabine can look really unusual. Even narrow chest of drawers can make useful storage place if the drawers a sectioned off so that the contents ca

get mixed up. A continuous work-
over the whole run of cabinets will
monize them.

iling the work surfaces makes an
ractive change from the usual
ninates. Remember to use specially
ghened tiles and an adhesive which
esistant to heat and water.

hop around for space-saving ideas
use inside the cupboards. Carousel
kets and plate racks, for example,
only make the most of cupboard
ce but also make it easier to get at
things inside. Deep basket drawers
be used to store bulky objects or
n act as vegetable racks.

An ordinary bookshelf placed on top
of a chest of drawers makes an
attractive dresser. If there is no room
for it in the kitchen, the dresser will
look equally good in a living room
where it can be used to store and
display such things as crockery,
cutlery and glassware.

An old broom handle can be varnished or painted and fitted with
decorative ends to look like a curtain
pole. You can then screw it on to the
wall and use it for hanging and dis-
playing kitchen untensils. Open-plan
display looks very decorative and
gives the kitchen an identity of its own,

## Safety hints

Safety is an important consideration in the kitchen. Although this
is where a high proportion of
accidents happen, careful planning
can help prevent most of them.

1. Keep cupboard doors shut—
somebody could get hurt walking
into one.
2. Do not let steam pour onto
electrical sockets.
3. Store sharp knives somewhere
inaccessible to children.
4. A small child could cut himself
on tins left in pedal bins.
5. Turn pan handles inwards so
children cannot pull them over.
6. Curtains and cloths near a
stove are a fire risk. Try to position
the stove away from the window.
7. Clean up immediately anything
spilt on the floor.
8. Trailing electrical flexes are
dangerous.
9. Everyday foods should not be
placed out of easy reach.
10. Do not overload sockets nor
site them too close to the sink.
11. Put sharp utensils away after
use.
12. Poisonous products must be
stored well away from a child's
reach.
13. Someone could easily trip over
things left on the floor.
14. Keep pets away from food.

Bill McLoughlin

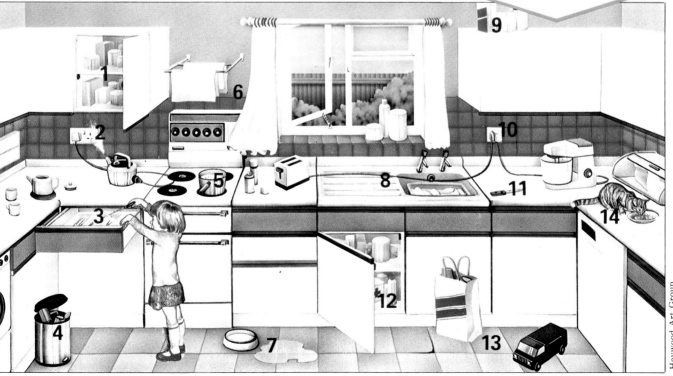

Haywood Art Group

# Flap-down breakfast table

Gavin Cochrane

It takes only a few basic materials to make this attractive flap-down table. And the snap-lock hinge makes it strong enough to bear the weight of all the essentials of a meal for two.

When not in use, the table takes up no space at all—which makes it a practical proposition for even the smallest of kitchens. Of course, if your kitchen is wide enough, the table could be left up to display, for instance, a colourful bowl of fruit. But its beauty lies in its versatility.

Covered in heat-resistant laminate, even a hot coffee or tea pot will not damage it. And a quick wipe-down leaves it looking as good as new.

Although shown here as a fold-away breakfast bar, this flap-down table could also be used in other rooms to make an unobtrusive yet accessible

**Above:** *The completed table*
**Right:** *Unobtrusive when not in use*
**Below:** *The simple, strong hinge*

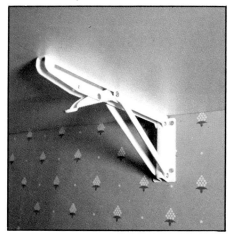

work surface. In a sewing room example, the table is more th strong enough to bear the weight o sewing machine. All you must do check for strength the wall to whi you are fixing the table. A plasterboa partition wall, for instance, is not ideal location.

Snap-lock hinges, which make th flap-down table so easy to use, a widely available from DIY stores, a though their exact design may va according to which type you buy.

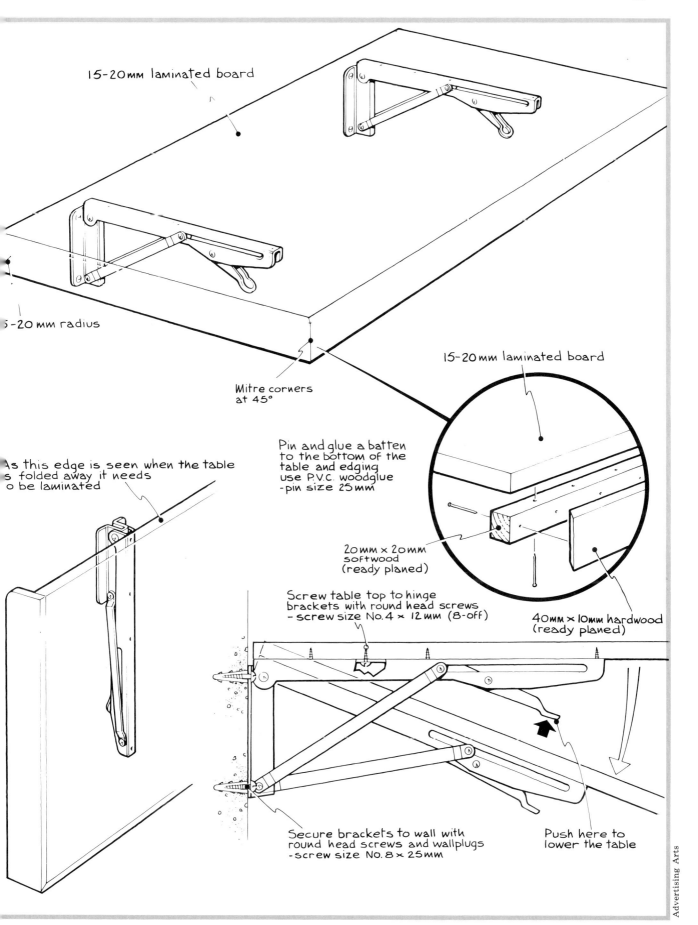

15-20mm laminated board

5-20 mm radius

Mitre corners
at 45°

As this edge is seen when the table
s folded away it needs
o be laminated

15-20mm laminated board

Pin and glue a batten
to the bottom of the
table and edging
use P.V.C. woodglue
-pin size 25mm

20mm × 20mm
softwood
(ready planed)

40mm × 10mm hardwood
(ready planed)

Screw table top to hinge
brackets with round head screws
- screw size No. 4 × 12mm (8-off)

Secure brackets to wall with
round head screws and wallplugs
-screw size No. 8 × 25mm

Push here to
lower the table

# Gluing and cramping

Types of glue and adhesive ● Which glue to use
for the job ● Different types of cramping device
explained ● How to apply glue to woodwork ●
Making a web cramp ● Cramping techniques

**Below**: *You can improvise a cram*
*for simple gluing jobs simply by us*
*terylene cord and a short piece of*
*dowel—which is used as a turn-ke*
*to tighten the web*

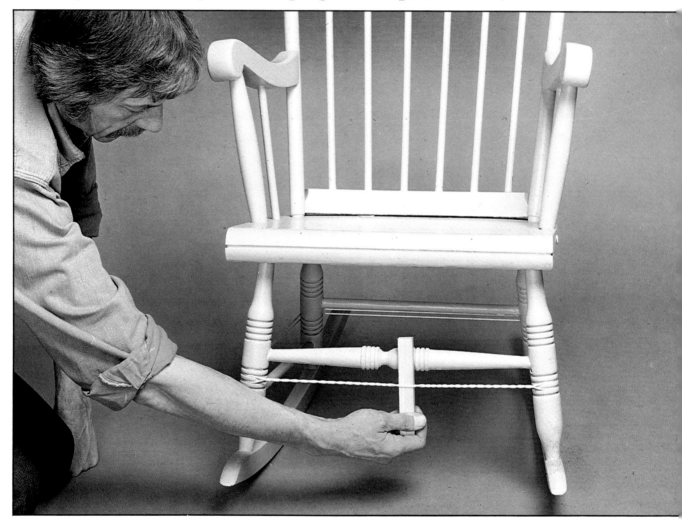

Modern adhesives have made it possible for amateur carpenters to construct wooden furniture which in the past only skilled craftsmen could have tackled. Work which would have once needed precise joints can now be joined simply with strong wood adhesive—using cramps to hold the wood in place while this is drying. You can choose from a variety of different cramps according to the wood size.

The term glue properly refers to pure animal or vegetable glue. Other types, which are resin based, are known as adhesives. The success of your gluing depends on choosing the right kind of glue for the job from the many different types available.

### Choosing the right adhesive

The glue or adhesive you use will depend on the type of wood you want to join together, the surface conditions, the kind of stress the join will be subjected to and whether a temporary or permanent join is wanted.

Pay particular attention to the temperature in the workshop. Most adhesives need a warm atmosphere in which to set. Make allowances too, for hard or resinous woods: these require a sap-resistant adhesive.

### Polyvinyl Acetate (PVA)

PVA adhesive is among the most useful for general-purpose woodwork. Available ready mixed in easy-to-use

plastic bottles, it is applied directly the wood which is then cramped. normal room temperatures, the sett time varies from 30 minutes to th hours depending on the brand used

Although PVA is a strong adhes and does not stain timber, it is completely waterproof and will adhere very readily to resinous or v hard wood such as teak. It is suitable for outdoor work.

Diluted with 20% water, PVA ca used to apply wood veneers. Damp veneer with a sponge and apply PVA evenly over the surfaces wit brush. Position the veneer then pl a sheet of brown paper on the and iron over it with a medium iro

### ...ea formaldehyde adhesive

...s is a good adhesive for hard, ...nous woods. Its gap-filling proper... ...also make it ideal for gluing loose... ...ng joints—such as those found in ...niture making and repairs. It ...sts moisture better than PVA.

### ...sorcinol formaldehyde

...s woodwork adhesive provides the ...atest strength and is the most ...er resistant, so it is ideal for out... ...r work and boatbuilding. It is also ...ood gap-filling adhesive.

...When adhesives have to be applied ...timber treated with preservative, ...urea formaldehyde or resorcinol.

### ...imal glue (Scotch glue)

...s is old fashioned glue made from ...mal pelts and bones. It comes both ...cake or granular form and in liquid ...n. The cake or granular varieties ...d to be melted down in a glue pot ...h water at a temperature of 65°C ...used while still hot. These do not ...in timber and dry to a medium ...wn colour which matches most ...ished or stained woods. They are ...waterproof.

...Unlike the granular variety, liquid ...mal glues can be used cold. Again ...y are not waterproof and do stain ...ne woods—especially oak—so ex... ...s glue should be wiped off with a ...np cloth before it can do any ...nage to the wood.

...nimal glue has largely been made ...olete by more modern adhesives ...is still the best to use when con... ...ucting frameworks for upholstered ...niture. The stresses which the ...me undergoes while being uphol... ...red may cause adhesive-made joints ...fracture.

...or mending or renovating antique ...niture, use an alburnum (sapwood) ...ed Scotch glue. This has the same ...ansion and contraction rate as old... ...hioned Scotch glue, which is differ... ...to that of modern adhesives. ...ver mix old and new glue on one ...ce of furniture.

### ...sein glues

...ese glues are now quite difficult to ...and have largely been replaced by ...a formaldehydes. Casein glues are ...de from milk and are available in ...vder which you mix with water. ...ey are water resistant when set but ...in a lot of timbers.

### ...nthetic resin cements

...is type of adhesive is almost ...npletely waterproof and comes in a ...iety of forms—powder, semi-liquid

or two parts (adhesive and hardener). It can be used for outdoor work and small boat-building. The setting time depends on the temperature of the surroundings—the warmer the air around the workpiece the faster it sets.

### Impact (or contact) adhesives

Wood stuck to wood with this type of adhesive tends to move after a time. It is therefore not strong enough for furniture making and is better suited to fixing laminates and tiles.

The surfaces to be stuck together are both coated with the impact adhesive and are then left to dry separately according to the manufacturer's instructions. Afterwards, the two surfaces are brought together to make an instant, strong bond.

Impact and contact adhesives are the only types which do not require cramping while they set. But as a bond is formed instantly, you should ensure that the mating surfaces are aligned.

### Epoxies

Almost any material can be stuck with epoxy adhesives but for woodworking, PVA and formaldehyde adhesives often prove to be both cheaper and easier to use. Epoxies are made up of two parts—a resin and a hardener— which must be mixed together. Setting time can vary between one hour and 24 hours.

### Cyanocrylate adhesives

Extra care must be taken when using these new 'super glues'. Manufacturers claim that one small spot of the adhesive and a little pressure will stick almost anything to anything in just a few moments. They will certainly stick skin to skin permanently, so be careful and make sure that children do not get anywhere near them.

---

### Safety precautions

Many adhesives are highly inflammable and some also give off toxic fumes. Make sure that you work in a well ventilated space and that there are no naked flames about.

Anyone who is prone to dermatitis should wear gloves or a barrier cream as glues contain skin irritants. If the glue should get on to unprotected skin and cause burns or an allergy rash, seek medical advice. If it gets in your eyes, wash it out with plenty of warm water and, again, seek medical advice.

---

## Types of cramp

The type of cramp you should use depends on the size of the wood you are gluing.

**G cramps:** The most versatile type of cramp, this gets its name from its shape which is like the letter G (fig. A). G cramps have a mouth capacity of between 25mm and 250mm or 300mm and are mainly used for cramping pieces of wood to a bench and for holding down veneer or laminate while the adhesive dries.

Variations on the basic G cramp include deep-mouthed cramps—which reach further across the workpiece— and small, sliding bar G cramps. The latter are smaller and easier to use than conventional G cramps and are useful for holding small pieces of timber in place.

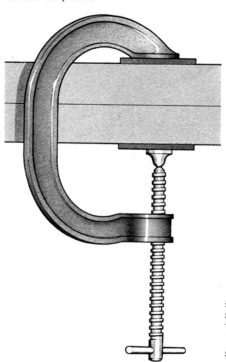

Bernard Fallon

**A.** *This G cramp is ideal when you want to hold smaller pieces of wood or awkward shapes as the glue sets*

**Sash cramps:** These are used to cramp larger pieces of timber, such as doors and window frames. Consisting of two adjustable stops on a long bar, they come in different lengths up to 3m long with extensions (fig. B). One stop is adjusted by sliding along the bar and securing with a pin: the other tightens like a vice jaw. Because of their size, sash cramps are expensive to buy. They are, however, obtainable from hire shops.

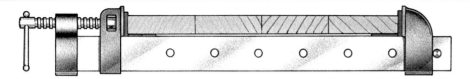

**Web cramp:** This consists of a 3.6m loop of nylon webbing, running through a ratchet, which can be tightened and released using a spanner or screwdriver (fig. 7). The web cramp cannot apply as much pressure as a sash cramp, but it is cheaper and is quite adequate for light and medium weight gluing jobs.

You can make an improvised form of web cramp by using strong cord and two short pieces of dowel (fig. 8). Tie a double thickness of the string around the object to be put under pressure then use the dowel to twist the strands together until the tension cramps the wood firmly. Use the second piece of dowel to hold the first in place.

## Preparation

If you are using liquid animal glue, make sure that it is fresh—most have a limited life and will cease to work properly if they are old.

Most, but not all, adhesives are effective only on surfaces which are free of moisture, dust and grease. Unless the instructions with your adhesive specify special gap-filling properties, the surfaces should also be reasonably smooth.

Always 'dry assemble' your work to begin with. Blow out dust from any

**B.** *Large scale gluing of things like long pieces of wood requires one or more sash cramps to hold the work really securely along its whole length while the glue is setting*

inaccessible corners of the work, then fit the pieces together. Having made the necessary adjustments and re-cleaned the joints, mark each part to eliminate the possibility of getting things in the wrong order on final assembly. Make sure that you sand and finish off any areas which would prove too inaccessible after gluing.

## Mixing and applying adhesives

Before you start mixing and applying your glue or adhesive, make sure that all the necessary cramping equipment is well to hand—it will be too late to search for it once the glue is mixed.

If there are any small holes or cracks in the wood, fill them at this stage. A good filler can be made by mixing a thin glue or adhesive with some sawdust: if you use sawdust from the same wood, the finished joint will be barely noticeable.

When making up a mixed glue or adhesive, use a small piece of wood and an old china teacup or saucer. Follow the manufacturer's instructions to the letter, taking particular care when water has to be added.

Use another, preferably flat, piece of wood to apply your glue or adhesive or apply it straight from the container. Again, you should follow the instructions carefully and make sure that each surface to be coated receives an

even covering. Glue invariably shri as it dries—causing stresses strains which will weaken the jc unless the coat is even.

## Cramping techniques

Unless you are using impact adhesi you should cramp the wood as soon the joint has been made. Whiche type of cramp you use, you must careful that the surface of the wo does not get scratched and dama by the action of the cramp while glue is setting. You can either some newspaper or alternatively, prevent the metal cramp jaws fr bruising the surface of the wo always ensure that there is a sm block of wood between the two (fig Make your blocks, or *cushions*, fr small offcuts. Keep them as clean a smooth as possible so that they do accidentally push the wood that being glued out of shape.

When using a G cramp, make su that the jaws and cushions are po tioned as far over the joint as possi (fig.3) then tighten the cramp finger-tight. Where two pieces angled, or wedge-shaped, wood being cramped, position a seco cramp at right-angles to the fi (fig. 5) to stop the parts slipping.

Use a sash cramp in the same way a G cramp, this time of course on larger scale. Make sure the sash exactly square to the workpiece distortions may result. During cran ing, the bar of the sash will tend bow in towards the workpiece, place small wedges underneath keep it straight.

When using a web cramp, or improvised alternative, ensure th the webbing runs around firmly fi parts of the workpiece. Otherwise, y may break one joint as you are tryi to cramp another.

If you are making an improvised w cramp, make sure that it is of a rea strong material like terylene cord.

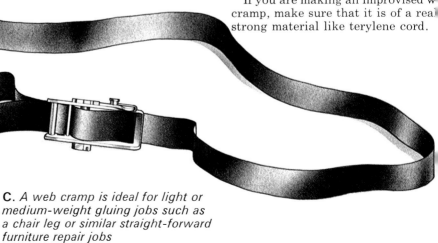

**C.** *A web cramp is ideal for light or medium-weight gluing jobs such as a chair leg or similar straight-forward furniture repair jobs*

**1** *Mix glue to the right consistency, if necessary, then apply it with a stick or straight from the glue bottle on to the surface of the wood*

**2** *With the wood on the bench wipe off any excess glue to prevent it staining and place the wood in whichever cramp you are using*

**3** *Place a block of wood between the wood you are gluing and the cramp to cushion the work and protect it while it is in the cramp*

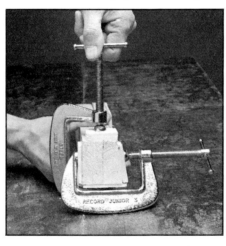

**4** *Tighten the cramp and if any excess glue is squeezed out of the join wipe it away. Leave the wood in the cramp for the required time*

**5** *If cramping wedge-shaped pieces of wood together, use a second cramp at right-angles to the first to stop the wood slipping*

**6** *If gluing long pieces of wood, use several sash cramps on alternate sides of the wood. Protect it with cushion blocks and paper*

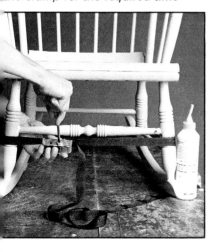

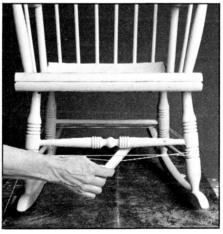

**7** *For light or medium-weight gluing jobs use a web cramp. Run the webbing through the ratchet and tighten steadily*

**8** *Make an improvised web cramp using terylene cord and a short piece of dowel. Use double-thickness cord around the object being glued*

**9** *Use the dowel to twist the strands together until the tension cramps the wood firmly. Use a second piece of dowel to hold the first*

Gavin Cochrane

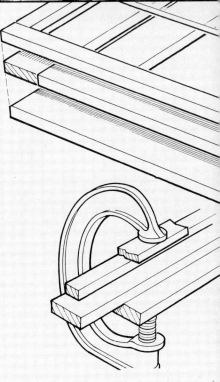

# Making a picture frame

This attractive wooden frame can easily be made in a few hours using only simple gluing and cramping techniques.

A variety of woods can be used to blend beautifully with any type of interior. The frame is ideal for enhancing the look of a modern picture or poster, or for giving an authentic look to old-fashioned prints. It can even be used for your family photographs—the design is flexible enough to suit whatever you want to display.

If you want to brighten up a dark corner of a room or hallway, consider putting in an ordinary mirror, secured to the back with special mirror bolts. The mirror also adds interest to a small, square room or makes a narrow hall look wider than it actually is.

If you hang the frame opposite a window where it can reflect the light, you will get an even more spacious feel. You could also hang the mirror in the bathroom with a simple fluorescent strip light above it to turn it into a shaving or make-up mirror.

Alternatively, add a touch of elegance to a room by hanging the frame with dark, smoked glass. While looking dramatic, it will still give the same reflection as ordinary mirror glass. Place some flowering plants by the mirror and their reflection will visually double the amount of flowers.

The frame shown here is made from commercial hardwood which has been stained. If you want a coloured frame, choose from the large variety of wood stains which are available. You can get wood stain and varnish combined or stain which is varnished separately to a matt or gloss finish. Alternatively you can stain the wood and then wax polish it.

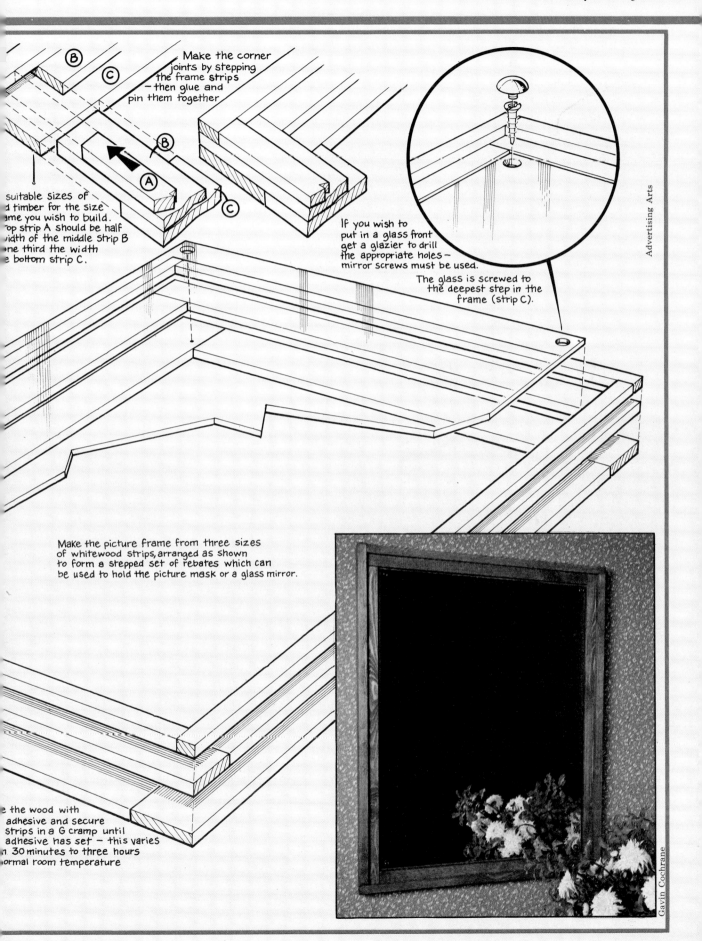

Make the corner joints by stepping the frame strips — then glue and pin them together

...suitable sizes of ...d timber for the size ...ame you wish to build. ...op strip A should be half ...idth of the middle strip B ...ne third the width ...e bottom strip C.

If you wish to put in a glass front get a glazier to drill the appropriate holes — mirror screws must be used.

The glass is screwed to the deepest step in the frame (strip C).

Make the picture frame from three sizes of whitewood strips, arranged as shown to form a stepped set of rebates which can be used to hold the picture mask or a glass mirror.

...e the wood with ...adhesive and secure ...strips in a G cramp until ...adhesive has set — this varies ...n 30 minutes to three hours ...ormal room temperature

Advertising Arts

Gavin Cochrane

# Glamorous make-up unit

**Suitable for either the bedroom or the bathroom this stylish make-up desk throws the maximum amount of light where it is needed most and provides plenty of storage space**

Built from easily-cleaned coated chipboard and pine this dressing table combines practical styling with a touch of Hollywood glamour. The side mirrors form two cupboard doors which can be opened and angled in for an all round view or left flat to provide eye-catching reflections.

The construction makes extens use of ready-made and simple kit pa and all the panels are joined toget by fixing blocks to minimize amount of screwing and drilling t must be done.

All the illustrated building acc sories are readily available fr hardware shops and timber mercha and they greatly simplify the task putting the dressing table together

106

## Cutting list

| Part | Material | No. | Size |
|---|---|---|---|
| **Leg Frame** | | | |
| uprights | 75 × 32 softwood (PAR) | 4 | 700 |
| cross rails | 75 × 32 softwood (PAR) | 4 | 390 |
| foot rails | 50 × 32 softwood (PAR) | 1 | 1396 |
| dowels | 12mm hardwood dowel | 16 | 50 |
| **Table Assembly** | | | |
| top | 25mm chipboard | 1 | 1412 × 533 |
| thickness battens | 75 × 32 softwood (PAR) | 1 | 1322 |
| thickness battens | 75 × 32 softwood (PAR) | 3 | 368 |
| sides | 150mm melamine faced chipboard | 2 | 513 × 135 |
| back | 150mm melamine faced chipboard | 1 | 1322 × 135 |
| drawer fronts | 150 melamine faced chipboard | 3 | 448 × 132 |
| side fixed runs | to suit drawer section | 2 | 428 |
| top hung runner | to suit drawer section | 4 | 428 |
| drawers | 100mm plastic drawer section | to suit type used. 4 sets | |
| drawer corners | | 4 sets | |
| drawer bases | 4mm melamine faced hardboard | to fit drawers | |
| plastic laminate | size shown allows for trim | | |
| plastic laminate ends | | 2 | 536 × 28 |
| plastic laminate front | | 1 | 1418 × 28 |
| plastic laminate top | | 1 | 1420 × 538 |
| channel clip on edging | | 6 | 448 |

| Part | Material | No. | Size |
|---|---|---|---|
| **Mirror faced cupboards** | | | |
| top and bottom | 150mm melamine faced chipboard | 2 | 1412 × 150 |
| centre uprights | 150mm melamine faced chipboard | 2 | 745 × 120 |
| end pieces | 150mm melamine faced chipboard | 2 | 745 × 130 |
| shelves | 225mm melamine faced chipboard | 5 | 337 × 116 |
| doors | 762mm melamine faced chipboard | 2 | 742 × 358 |
| centre front | 762mm melamine faced chipboard | 1 | 745 × 690 |
| mirrors for door | 4mm ground edge mirror | 2 | 740 × 350 |
| centre mirror | 4mm ground edge mirror | 1 | 740 × 350 |
| backing | 4mm melamine faced hardboard | 1 | 1409 × 773 |
| backing edging | 4mm × 15mm plastic hockey stick tape | 2 | 775 |
| | | 1 | 1412 |
| switch | architrave switch | 1 | |

**Additional materials:** Knock-down fittings, contact adhesive, shelf fittings, 5 amp 3-core heat-resistant cable, PVA adhesive, pins, chipboard screws, white chipboard iron-on edging.

**NB** all exposed chipboard edges to be covered with iron-on edging strip.

All sizes are in millimetres and all the leg frame sizes refer to timber which has been planed all round (PAR sizes).

# Workplan

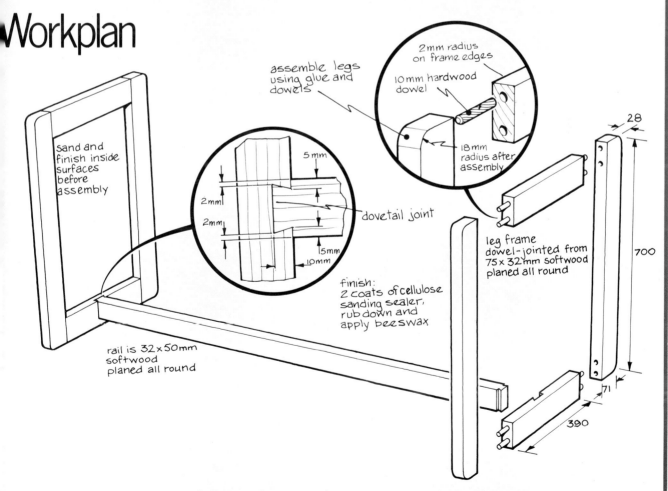

sand and finish inside surfaces before assembly

assemble legs using glue and dowels

2mm radius on frame edges

10mm hardwood dowel

18mm radius after assembly

2mm

2mm

5mm

5mm

10mm

dovetail joint

finish: 2 coats of cellulose sanding sealer, rub down and apply beeswax

leg frame dowel-jointed from 75 × 32mm softwood planed all round

28

700

71

390

rail is 32 × 50mm softwood planed all round

**Above, left :** *After assembly plane the leg surfaces flush and chamfer the edge to a 2mm radius. Mark the 18mm corner radius with a soft pencil and compasses*

*before shaping with a rasp or chisel. Finish with medium grade glasspaper.* **Above, right :** *The stop dovetail housing adds strength to the bottom rail*

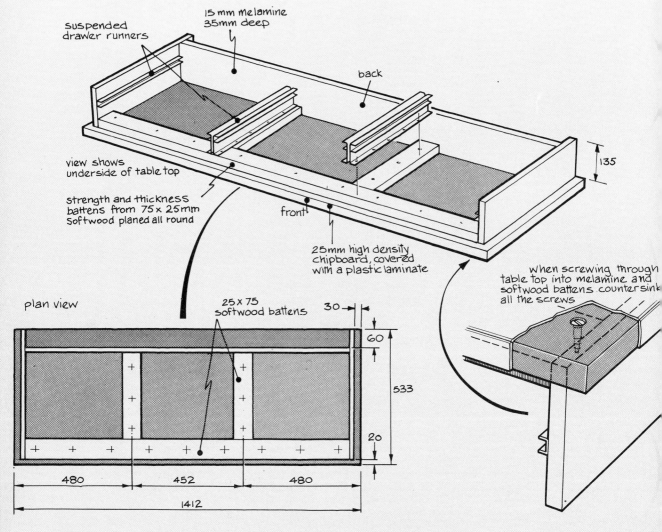

suspended drawer runners

15 mm melamine 35mm deep

back

view shows underside of table top

135

strength and thickness battens from 75 x 25mm softwood planed all round

front

25mm high density chipboard, covered with a plastic laminate

when screwing through table top into melamine and softwood battens countersink all the screws

plan view

25 x 75 softwood battens

30

60

533

20

480

452

480

1412

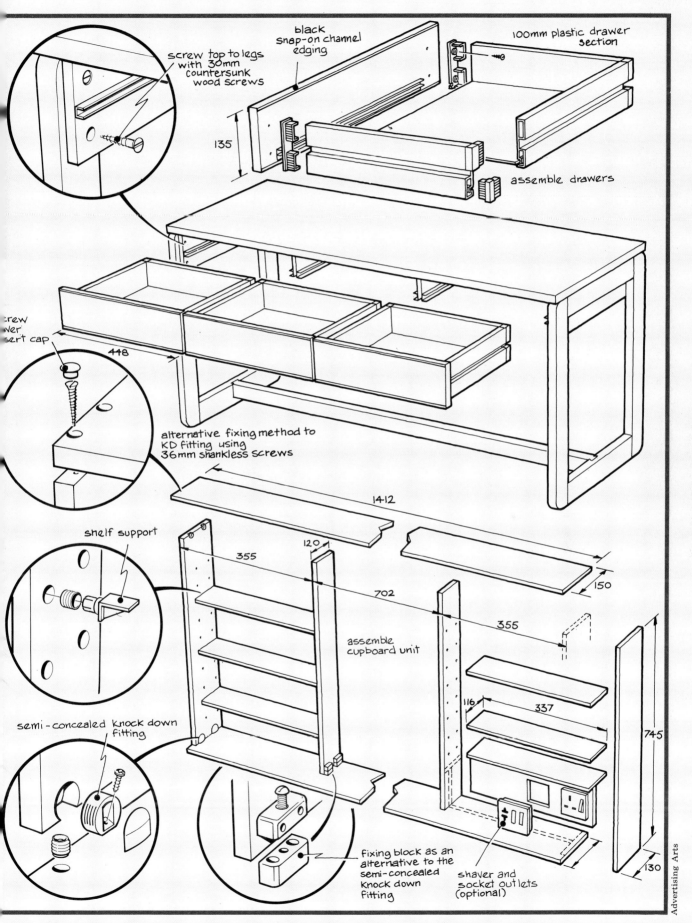

screw top to legs with 30mm countersunk wood screws

black snap-on channel edging

100mm plastic drawer section

135

assemble drawers

screw drawer insert cap

448

alternative fixing method to KD fitting using 36mm shankless screws

1412

shelf support

355

120

702

150

assemble cupboard unit

355

116

337

745

semi-concealed knock down fitting

fixing block as an alternative to the semi-concealed knock down fitting

shaver and socket outlets (optional)

130

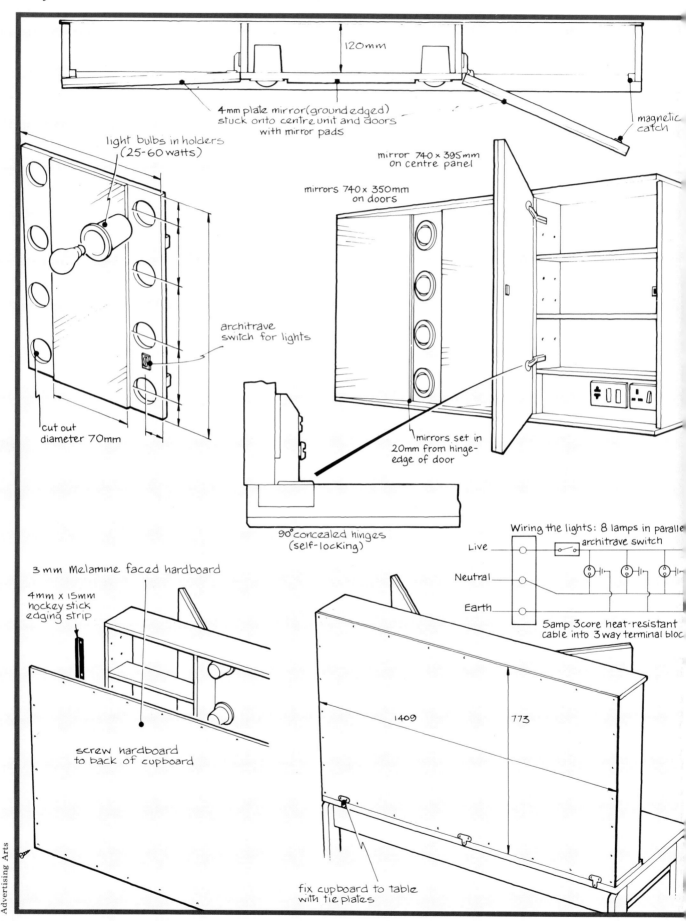

4mm plate mirror (grounded edged) stuck onto centre unit and doors with mirror pads

120mm

magnetic catch

light bulbs in holders (25-60 watts)

mirror 740 x 395mm on centre panel

mirrors 740 x 350mm on doors

architrave switch for lights

cut out diameter 70mm

mirrors set in 20mm from hinge-edge of door

90° concealed hinges (self-locking)

Wiring the lights: 8 lamps in parallel

Live
Neutral
Earth

architrave switch

5amp 3core heat-resistant cable into 3 way terminal bloc

3 mm Melamine faced hardboard

4mm x 15mm hockey stick edging strip

screw hardboard to back of cupboard

1409          773

fix cupboard to table with tie plates

# Painting interior woodwork

**Surface preparation ● Using a blowlamp ● Making good ● Which paint to use ● Painting doors ● The right way to set about skirtings and architraves ● Dealing with sash windows**

**Above**: *A light upward stroke of the brush will ensure that your painted surface is free from unsightly streaks and ridges*

Repainting the woodwork around the house will give your decoration a facelift for very little cost. And if you set about it the right way, you can be sure of a really professional finish.

**Preparing the surface**

Whether painting over new woodwork or a surface that has been painted previously, it is vital to make sure that the surface is sound, clean and dry.

With new woodwork, smooth the surface down with glasspaper, slightly rounding off any sharp edges. Treat knots or resinous patches with a proprietary knotting compound to prevent them from leaking sap through to the new paint. You can either buy this or make up your own from 70 parts of methylated spirit mixed with 30 parts shellac. Apply the knotting as accurately as possible, using a small brush or a pad of cloth wrapped round the finger. Fill cracks and open joints with a cellulose or resin filler.

To ensure that the paint adheres to the surface, new wood should be given a coat of primer. Primer also partially seals the wood surfaces, preventing leaking sap from spoiling the final coat of paint.

Check that the primer you use is suitable for the particular type of wood to be painted. Highly resinous wood should be treated with aluminium wood primer which has very effective sealing qualities. If in doubt about which primer to use for a particular job, consult your paint dealer.

In most cases, previously painted woodwork needs no more than cleaning and lightly rubbing down to prepare it. Remove all dirt and grease by washing the surface with warm water and detergent or sugar soap, paying particular attention to areas on doors which are handled often and to wax polished surfaces. If dirt and wax deposits are not removed, they may cause paint to dry slowly and lose its final gloss appearance.

If the paintwork has been particularly exposed to grease, in a kitchen for example, use a proprietary paint cleaner. Rinse off with plenty of clean water and allow the surface to dry.

To key the surface for the new paint, old gloss must be abraded to remove its shine. Although glasspaper can be used for this, better results are obtained with wet and dry paper—an abrading paper which, when used wet, gives a very smooth finish.

Use a medium grade of paper—wrapped around a wood or cork block—and rub firmly with the grain (fig.1).

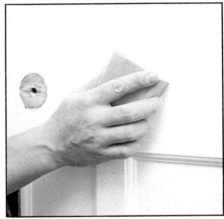

**1** *When treating woodwork that has been previously painted, abrade the old gloss to remove its shine and provide a key for the new paint*

**2** *When the old paintwork has been sanded, wipe over it with a cloth dampened in white spirit to remove any traces of dust and grease*

John Ward

**3** *Remove any flaws on the surface of old paintwork, such as flaking paint around removed door fittings, with a paint scraper*

**4** *Paint on the areas around window frames and glass panels in doors often flakes. Scrape off as much of the old paint as possible*

**5** *Use a paint brush to apply primer to any areas that are chipped or dented, or where old paint has been stripped altogether*

**6** *Use cellulose filler to fill in any chips and dents in the wood, so that the damaged areas are brought up level with the existing paintwork*

**7** *When the cellulose filler is dry, smooth the area with glasspaper wrapped around a wood or cork block, then prime the area again*

cloth dampened in white spirit (fig or use tack-rag—cloth impregnat with slow-drying varnish—which specifically designed for the purpo Leave the woodwork to dry befo you begin to paint.

**Dealing with damaged surface**
Unless a damaged surface is thoroug ly prepared beforehand, flaws such blisters and bubbles will be acce tuated and may spoil the finish.

Blisters and bubbles are usua caused by pockets of moisture or re which become trapped beneath t surface of the original paint coat. U a sharp knife to cut out the blister paint, smooth off the hard paint edg with glasspaper then treat the ar with multi-purpose primer.

Large or resinous knots and sm resinous patches in woodwork shou be treated with a knotting compoun

Flaking paint is most likely to found on window frames which ha been affected by the weather and condensation. Remove as much of t loose paint as possible with a pai scraper or sharp knife (fig.4). Smoo down the area with glasspaper un all the remaining paint is quite soun Any knots that have been exposed this process should be dealt with described above.

Cracks occur when wood joints ha dried out or split. The most commo problem areas are window frame architraves—the mouldings arou doors and windows—and the corn joints in skirting. Start by widenir the cracks with a sharp knife, rakir out any dust and dirt as you go. Prir the enlarged cracks and plug the with cellulose filler (fig.6). When dr smooth with glasspaper (fig.7) a prime with a multi-purpose primer.

Particularly large or deep crac

**8** *Use a paint-stripping head when stripping paint with a blowlamp. Play the flame from side to side to avoid charring the wood*

**9** *Use a shave hook when stripping mouldings. To prevent shreds of melting paint from falling onto your hand, hold the tool at an angle*

Rinse the paper in water as it becomes clogged with old paint and remove muddy build-ups from the woodwork with a sponge and clean water. If a particularly smooth finish is required

—such as on a flush door—run over the surface again with a fine grade of wet and dry or glasspaper.

To remove the last specks of dust and grease, wipe the surface over with

uld be filled in layers. Allow each
er of filler to dry before you start
apply the next.

Chips and dents develop through
eral wear and tear. Correct them
you would blisters and bubbles,
ng cellulose filler to level up the
as with the outer paint coat. When
, sand smooth and prime.

## ripping paint

a painted surface is particularly
ly damaged, strip the paint off
npletely. Although paint can be
pped using just a paint scraper,
s can become tiring over large
as. More efficient methods are
mical stripping (see pages 15-19) or
t stripping with a blowlamp and
aper. However, do not strip window
nes with a blowlamp as the heat
y crack the glass.

f you decide to use a blowlamp, buy
pecial paint-stripping head which
eads the flame over a wider area
.8). Use a waste tin to catch the
ces of hot paint. Protect the floor
h an asbetos sheet rather than with
vspaper or a dustsheet.

Begin stripping at the bottom of an
a and work upwards, covering only
mall area at a time. Play the flame
m side to side to avoid burning the
nt and charring the wood. As the
nt melts, scrape it off holding the
aper at an angle so that shreds of
paint do not fall on to your hand.
r stripping mouldings, use a shave
ok (fig.9). When all the paint has
n stripped off, prime the bare wood.

## dercoats

ou are painting new wood that has
y been primed, or over paintwork
a different colour, it is advisable to
ly an undercoat to provide a good
for the final coat of gloss. Check
paint charts when buying the gloss
undercoat to make sure they
tch. Leave the undercoat until
—the manufacturer's recommended
ing time will be given on the tin—
ore applying the gloss top coat.

## oss paint

erior woodwork is traditionally
nted with gloss paint. Doors,
rtings and window frames all take
te a few knocks and gloss paint
nds up to hard wear better than
ulsion—as well as being easier to
an with a damp cloth.

raditional gloss paint is oil-based
includes resin to give it hard
aring qualities. Acrylic paint is
vater-based gloss which is jelly-like
consistency, and does not drip. It

**10** *To ensure that no brush mark is left on finished paintwork, 'lay off' the paint by running the brush upwards with a very light stroke*

**12** *When painting panels, start brush strokes from the edges and work towards the middle. Blend the edges to eliminate overlap marks*

should never be stirred, however, as
this will reduce its non-drip qualities
and hence its advantages.

### Brush strokes

If applied incorrectly, gloss shows up
blemishes and brush marks more than
any other type of paint. It is therefore
vital to use proper brush strokes.

Apply ordinary gloss quickly, evenly
and in as full a coat as possible. Using
acrylic paint, apply a little at a time
and take care not to overbrush or
runs will occur. For small areas of
woodwork, your brush strokes should
always run the same way as the grain
of the wood. In large areas, brushing
in three different directions will help
you obtain a smoother finish.

Start by applying the paint in a
random way, criss-crossing the brush:
when a section has been covered, draw
the brush over the paint horizontally.
Finally, 'lay off' the paint by running
the brush upwards over the paint very
lightly so that no mark is left (fig.10).

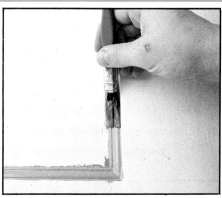

**11** *For mouldings on panel doors, use a 12mm brush. Apply the paint sparingly so that it does not accumulate in ugly ridges.*

**13** *To keep paint off glass, protect it with a paint shield. If paint does get onto the glass, wait for it to dry, then scrape it off*

John Ward

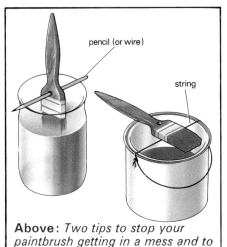

pencil (or wire)

string

**Above:** *Two tips to stop your paintbrush getting in a mess and to keep the bristles in perfect condition*

### Painting doors

Doors are not as easy to paint as
you might think. To make the job
easier, start by wedging the door base
against the floor with a small piece of

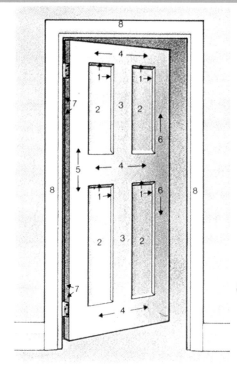

**A.** *The painting sequence for a panel door. Panel doors should be painted in one session without pauses*

wood. This will stop it from swinging shut, and perhaps ruining a wet edge. Remove as much metalwork as you can including handles, knobs and key escutcheons.

When painting flush doors, start at the top and work down in rectangular sections using a 75mm brush. Work quickly so that the paint does not harden before you have completed an adjoining section. Blend the sections carefully as you go, to eliminate any overlap marks.

Apply the paint by making two or three separate down strokes. Without reloading the brush, fill in any gaps by cross brushing then gently lay off the paintwork. When you are painting the edge of the door, use a brush slightly narrower than the width of the edge. If you use a wider brush, paint is likely to run down the front and back surfaces of the door.

Panel doors should be painted in a strict sequence (fig.A) and in one session—any pauses will result in the formation of a hard edge which is almost impossible to remove.

When painting mouldings, use a 12mm brush to work the paint well in-to each corner (fig.11). Do not overload the brush or paint will accumulate in ugly ridges. As you paint each panel, always work from the outside towards the middle (fig.12).

## Skirting and architraves

Start painting skirting at the top edge and architraves at the edge where they meet the wall.

To brush up, or 'cut in' to the wall at this point, use a cutting-in tool— a specially angled brush—or a 25mm brush on its side. Avoid overloading the brush—dipping it only about 13mm into the paint—and cut in with one, continuous stroke.

If walls are to be papered, extend the paintwork about 10mm up the wall above the skirting.

Paint the remaining parts of skirt-ings and architraves with a wider brush—50mm or 75mm—following the grain of the wood.

**B.** *To 'cut in' where a skirting board or an architrave meets the wall, use a shaped cutting-in tool*

## Windows

The paintwork on wooden windows must be kept in good condition if the frames are to be prevented from rotting. You should therefore take the opportunity of painting the top and under edges of any opening frame at the same time as the visible ones.

Remove any window fittings such as sash fasteners and make sure that the surface is clean and sound. Clean the glass, to prevent any dust or dirt on it from falling on to the wet paint.

To keep paint off the glass, mask up each pane. This is best done with an aluminium or plastic paint shield (fig.13)—obtainable from DIY shops— or use masking tape instead. If paint still penetrates on to the glass, wait until it is dry then scrape it off with a paint scraper or a sharp knife.

Casement windows, like panel doors, should be painted in a strict sequence (fig.C). Paint in the direction of the grain and use a cutting-in tool, or narrow brush on its side, to cut in where the paint meets the wall and the window pane.

To paint a sash window, begin by pulling the bottom sash up and the top sash down to expose the meeting rail. When the bottom parts of the top sash have been painted, almost close the window then paint the remaining areas (fig. D). Finish off in the order shown for casement windows.

For safety at each stage of painting, fix the sashes in position with a small wooden wedge. Wait until the paint is

quite dry before closing the window c it may stick fast.

When you come to the runner: remember that only those section that are visible when the window open need be painted—the rest ar amply protected from the weather b the tight fit of the window sashe: Take care though, not to get paint o the sash cords, as it will weaken then

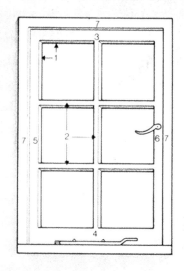

**C.** *Casement windows should be painted in a strict sequence. Paint the top and under edges of the frame as well as the visible areas*

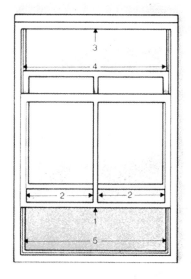

**D.** *The painting sequence for a sash window. Finish off in the order shown for casement windows*

# Dress up your doors

Most people paint their doors in single, plain colours. But, with a little imagination and the use of different colours and designs, a dull door can be made to enhance the appearance of a room. On panel doors you can paint the panels and mouldings in different colours or, if preferred, in differing shades of the same colour. Stripes and designs can be painted onto flush and panel doors, with the use of masking tape, and extended across the adjacent walls. For a really modern look, try painting a design onto a door that matches, and draws attention to, a nearby picture on the wall.

Skirting boards can also be painted imaginatively to liven up the look of a room. For instance, if you decide to paint a coloured stripe across or around a door, try painting the skirting board in the same colour or a matching shade. Here are just a few ideas that can brighten and enliven the interior woodwork of your home.

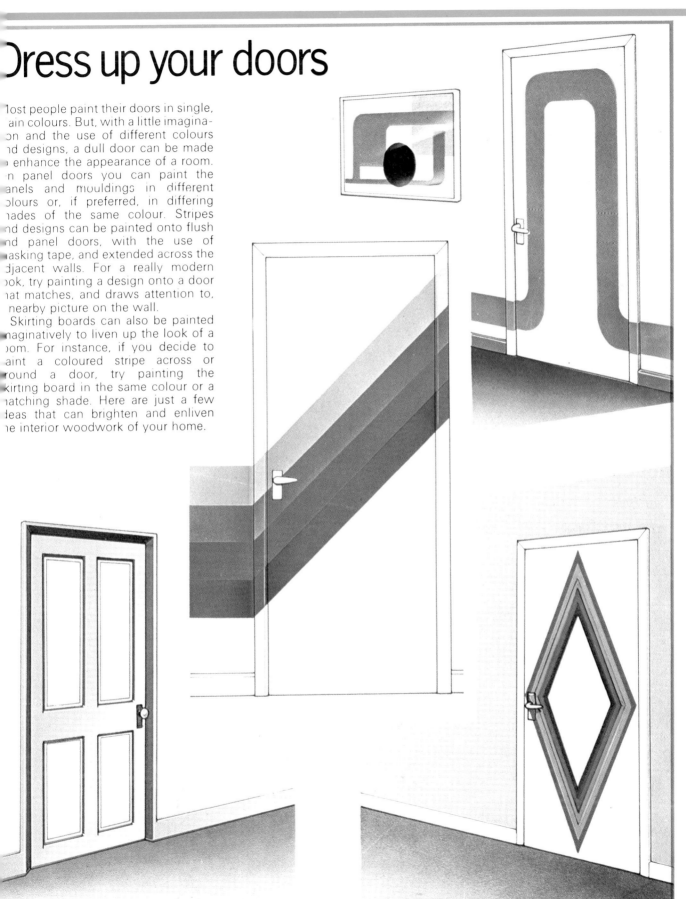

# Keeping the heat in

**Heat loss around the house ● Jobs you can do yourself ● Insulating the loft ● Choosing the right insulating materials ● Calculating quantities ● Filling in awkward corners**

About three-quarters of all heating in an uninsulated house is lost to the atmosphere, much of it through the roof (fig. A). Insulating your roof space is a cheap way of counteracting this loss and will noticeably cut your heating bills.

Although insulation against heat loss or gain is now considered an essential requirement for all homes, most houses are not as well insulated as they should be for maximum economy and comfort. Also remember insulation helps keep the house cool in summer.

Regardless of the exact type material used by the house builde there is nearly always room for im provement. And because of fast-risin fuel costs, in the long run you wi save money whatever the actual co and quantity of your insulation.

### Insulating materials
The cheapest and simplest way insulating the loft is to place insula ting material between, or over, th ceiling joists. Various types of natura and man-made material are availabl either in rolled blankets or in granu lated form. But as there is little t choose between them in terms c effectiveness you should base you choice on the cost and selection c what is available locally.

Mineral-fibre or glassfibre mattin and blanket comes in roll form, cu to fit the average space between floo joists. On its own, this is normall adequate for insulating a roof: awk ward nooks and crannies can be fille with off-cuts from the rolls once th main insulation is laid.

**A.** *Typical heat losses and cold down-draughts in an uninsulated home*

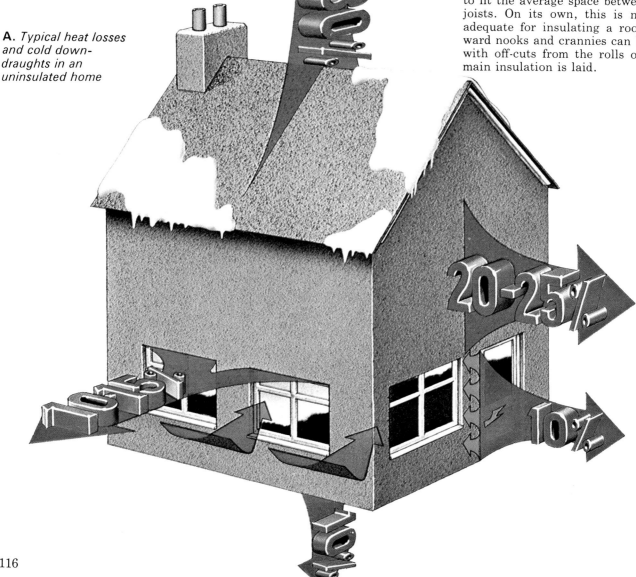

# A dozen ways to reduce heat loss

## Jobs for the specialists:

**1.** If the fireplace is no longer used, have the chimney stopped and vented to prevent an upwards draught

**2.** Some types of board or blanket insulation need to be fitted with care to prevent roof damage and excessive condensation

**3.** Spray-blown loft and cavity wall insulation are both extremely effective, but involve considerable expense

**4.** Insulation can be fitted above a false ceiling—useful when roof access is not possible

**5.** Sealed-unit double glazing has to be installed by a professional as some structural work is involved

**6.** Floor cavity insulation involves considerable turmoil unless laid at the time of building or when flooring repairs are made

## Jobs you can do yourself:

**7.** Some forms of blanket insulation can be tacked to the rafters and covered by hard or soft boarding

**8.** Insulation placed between the joists, a covering for this, and lagging of tanks and pipes are jobs easily done

**9.** Another inexpensive and effective insulation job is cutting out draughts around doors, windows and unused chimneys and fireplaces

**10.** A bigger job, cheaper than cavity insulation and almost as effective, is to panel insulate the inside of the outer leaf of a cavity wall

**11.** Secondary sash double glazing, provided in kit form, is usually easily fitted to conventional windows

**12.** Thicker fitted floor coverings not only look good, but help greatly to prevent continuous heat loss

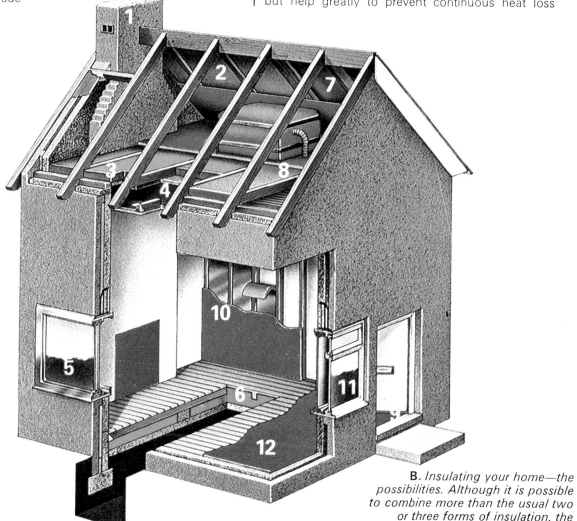

**B.** *Insulating your home—the possibilities. Although it is possible to combine more than the usual two or three forms of insulation, the cost-effectiveness of the final combination is worth considering*

However, in older houses, where the ceiling joists are likely to be more narrowly spaced than is usual today, laying a standard-width roll material is a laborious task—every bit has to be tucked in at the edges. In this case, loose-fill insulation is much easier to work with.

Loose fill comes in bags, either in granule form or as pieces of loose fibre. Among the materials used are polystyrene, vermiculite—an expandable mica—and mineral wool (rock wool). The latter is also available made up into blanket rolls.

Besides being handy where the space between floor joists is narrow, loose-fill insulates inaccessible corners more effectively than offcuts of rolled material. In draughty lofts however, the granules blow about unless the floor joists are covered over. Insulation problems are often best solved by using roll for the main body of the floor and loose-fill around the edge of the loft. The roll form makes laying an easy job if the separation of the joists is not too narrow.

Whichever type of material is chosen and however this is laid, depth of insulation is the crucial factor. About 100mm is considered a satisfactory compromise between cost and effectiveness. Roll materials are available in thicknesses of about 75mm or 80mm for topping up existing insulation, and of about 100mm for dealing with a loft which has no insulation.

### Calculating quantities

Inspecting the loft gives you a chance to estimate both the quantity of material required and the extent of work involved. To help you move around, and to avoid accidentally damaging the ceiling below, place stout planks across the floor joists.

To gauge the amount of material needed, measure the length and width of the loft then calculate the overall floor space. Against this, allow for the space taken up by obstacles such as storage tanks and large beams.

If you are considering adding to existing insulation, think in terms of bringing it up to the 100mm depth of loose-fill or blanket insulation recommended for uninsulated roofs.

A typical roll of blanket material of 100mm depth measures about 6.25m in length. 'Topping up' rolls, with depths of about 75mm or 80mm, are slightly longer at about 8m—and usually more expensive. The easiest way of working out your needs is to add together the total length of the strips of ceiling to be covered, and divide this by the length of the roll material you are using to do the job.

Add to this number of rolls a generous surplus to take care of trimming and overlap. Remember to allow for the turn up at the eaves if you think this is advisable, and add any extra for the water tank, its piping, and the trapdoor.

If you are using loose-fill material, your requirements are best based on the manufacturer's own tables and recommendations—on the assumption you will be adding insulation up to the depth of 100mm.

While you are in the loft, inspect the flashings which exclude water at the junction of the roof and other surfaces, such as around the chimney.

On no account should you proceed with insulation if there is any evidence of roof leakage or wet rot, as loft insulation can aggravate both these problems considerably.

At the same time, take a look at the electrics. Wiring perishes in time—especially the older cloth-covered rubber-insulated type—and in any case may not take kindly to repeated knocks while you are laying the insulating material.

The illustration shows the va ways of insulating, on the lef unused loft and, on the right, an in the process of being conve Although the basic forms of insul materials are identical for each, are used in slightly different ways

Blanket insulation is inexpe and effective and in most instance roll ends need only be taken up t joist end or wall-plate (1) but will to be folded up against the roof draughts are excessive. Roll the bl inwards from the eaves, allowi generous overlap where a new le meets old (2).

Other uses for blanket materia clude lining and draughtproofir the loft door (3) and between r (4). A double thickness furthe proves insulation, being partic effective for sound proofing a floor (5) that forms part of a conversion. It is important tha insulation is laid directly beneat water tank (6), even if the loft a used as a living room. The water need not be otherwise insulate this instance.

Loose-fill 'rock wool' or vermi is much more convenient for ins ing a 'bitty' ceiling, in areas well cl draughts (8). Again, increasing depth improves both heat and s insulation (9). The use of loose-f insulating within a water-tank b much more satisfactory than a de blanket lagging, but you will ha construct a softboard box (10) ar the tank.

Remember that any pipework open loft has to be lagged also. can use blanket insulation of hessian wrapping, preformed neo (11) or polystyrene tubing for the

A draughty roof can be insu with a special lined blanket ma placed between the rafters (12) is attached to the tile battens, the rafter sides by battening (13 material must be led clear of the ends to prevent any condens from seeping into a wall cavity.

The rafters can then be covered insulating softboard (14), and fin off with tempered plywood if n sary—particularly if the loft conve is for a living area—and this ca provided by blanket material (15 solid and easily worked slab polystyrene, rockwool or fibrebo

---

### Home Insulation Act 1978

Under the provisions of this Act, UK residents may qualify for a grant of 66% or £50—which ever is the less—towards the cost of insulating a loft. The grant is payable by your local authority providing certain straightforward conditions are met. One of these is that application for a grant is made prior to starting any work. The application procedure is simple and approval is normally very quick. Full details can be obtained from your local Council offices.

---

### Safety precautions

All types of fibre insulation give off fibre-dust and some people handling the material may experience skin irritation. This is normally a temporary nuisance and its effects can be minimized by not wearing tight clothing. By rinsing off the hands and body prior to soaping when washing down, you can avoid rubbing the fibres into the skin. Use additional protection, such as gloves and a handkerchief face-mask, when ripping and shaping material in confined spaces.

# Insulate your loft

same types of 'solid' insulation used on the party wall of two particularly where the other part is uninsulated. It is better to use insulation behind a false wall if rance is important and rising from next door poses a problem. flooring in a loft conversion can variety of forms but a chipboard dboard base is best (16). This e tiled or carpeted as desired, or re if additional material (5 and 9)

is used for sound insulation beneath.

In planning the conversion consider installing a professionally double-glazed window, or install a sealed-unit yourself (17). The roof is, afterall, usually the most exposed part of the house and the additional cost of double-glazing—if kept simple—is unlikely to have much effect on the overall cost of the conversion. If the conversion is to be used for living purposes—as a playroom or children's

bedroom—a double-glazed window should be installed for reasons of personal comfort alone.

If efficient underfloor insulation is installed (in part to act as sound insulation), rising heat from the house will not reach the loft area and additional heating must be provided.

So, if you do convert the space under the roof it is best to think about floor insulation first—it may not be necessary.

**1** Take blanket insulation right up to the wall plate at the eaves, and tuck in the edges at the joists if the blanket is too wide

**2** Where possible, tuck the insulation under obstructions. Note the use of a stout plank as a working platform

**3** Blanket material can be easily ⊂ to shape with large scissors or garden shears. Offcuts can be used for pipe lagging and elsewhere

John Ward

**4** Loose-fill material is a quick and effective way of dealing with awkward spots such as around the chimney stack and wiring boards

**5** Level off the loose-fill to the top of the joists. If these are very deep use a 'T'-shaped board cut to give the required depth of material

**6** Allow plenty of overlap when covering the loft door—this prevents draughts—and do not insulate beneath the water tank,

## Planning the work

When laying blanket insulation, it is infuriating to find that every roll ends short of the mark or repeatedly needs cutting at, say, a particularly large roof member—leaving an almost useless offcut.

The most convenient place for rolls to end is away from the eaves—it is difficult enough having to stretch into these inaccessible areas just to push the insulation home. You should therefore plan on working away from the eaves wherever possible. Any offcuts can be used up later to insulate a more accessible strip in the middle of the loft area.

## Laying materials

When you come to lay your insulation, simply follow the set pattern of joists across the roof. Loose-fill material can be levelled to the correct depth using a template made from thick card or wood off-cut. Shape this to fit the space between joists (fig.5). Like roll materials, loose-fill should be laid

working inwards from the eaves. Level the filling towards a clear space in the middle of the loft where addition and removal will present far less of a problem.

Roll material can be cut to length and shape with large scissors or slashed, carefully, with a handyman's knife. Awkward shapes are more conveniently torn from a supply length. Be generous in the cutting length so that you can tuck in the surplus at the end. Allow 100mm overlap when continuing with a fresh length. Where the two lengths join, either tightly butt the two ends or leave the excess to overlap by about 100mm. Offcuts can be used to fill small gaps between lengths.

In order to prevent the possible build-up of condensation, ventilation space must be left around the edges of the loft. Even so, strong draughts can be prevented by arranging for the roll ends to be turned up between the rafters—allow extra material for this if necessary. In most cases you need

insulate only as far as the wall-plat the barrier between the joists eaves (fig.1).

The loft area is finished off by sulating the access trap or door w spare lengths of rolled insulati glued, tied or tacked in place. Al the material to overspill when clos so that any draughts are excluded.

## Partial loft conversions

Boarding over the joists and raft after you have insulated the loft v reduce heat loss still further. L chipboard to form the new floor a tempered hardboard or fibreboard the ceiling.

Before covering the rafters, tack tie lengths of blanket roll to the battens in between. If this pro difficult, simply trap each length roll in place as you pin the ceil panel over it.

Where the loft has already be partially floored or panelled, rem as much as you can for access th force in loose-fill material.